FLORIDA

SCIENCE
Fusion

fusion [FYOO • zhuhn] a mixture or blend
formed by fusing two or more things

This Interactive Student Edition belongs to

_____

Teacher/Room

_____

HOUGHTON MIFFLIN HARCOURT

Consulting Authors

Michael A. DiSpezio
Global Educator
North Falmouth, Massachusetts

Marjorie Frank
*Science Writer and Content-Area Reading
   Specialist*
Brooklyn, New York

Michael Heithaus
*Director, School of Environment and Society
Associate Professor, Department of Biological
   Sciences*
Florida International University
North Miami, Florida

Donna Ogle
Professor of Reading and Language
National-Louis University
Chicago, Illinois

 HOUGHTON MIFFLIN HARCOURT

Front Cover: *lion cub* ©Cesar Lucas Abreu/Stone/Getty Images; *grass background* ©Nicholas Eveleigh/Stockbyte/Getty Images; *field of tulips* ©John McAnulty/Corbis; *soccer players* ©Jon Feingersh Photography Inc/Blend Images/Getty Images; *volcano* ©Westend61 GmbH/Alamy; *microscope* ©Thom Lang/Corbis.

Back Cover: *wind turbines* ©Comstock/Getty Images; *observatory* ©Robert Llewellyn/Workbook Stock/Getty Images; *giraffe* ©The Africa Image Library/Alamy; *guitar and saxophone* ©Brand Z/Alamy.

Printed in the U.S.A.

ISBN   978-0-547-33877-4

4 5 6 7 8 9 10 1421 19 18 17 16 15 14 13 12 11
4500290204   BCDEF

Program Advisors

Paul D. Asimow
*Professor of Geology and
    Geochemistry*
California Institute of Technology
Pasadena, California

Bobby Jeanpierre
*Associate Professor of Science
    Education*
University of Central Florida
Orlando, Florida

Gerald H. Krockover
*Professor of Earth and Atmospheric
    Science Education*
Purdue University
West Lafayette, Indiana

Rose Pringle
*Associate Professor
    School of Teaching and Learning*
College of Education
University of Florida
Gainesville, Florida

Carolyn Staudt
*Curriculum Designer for Technology
    KidSolve, Inc.*
The Concord Consortium
Concord, Massachusetts

Larry Stookey
Science Department
Antigo High School
Antigo, Wisconsin

Carol J. Valenta
*Senior Vice President and Associate
    Director of the Museum*
Saint Louis Science Center
St. Louis, Missouri

Barry A. Van Deman
President and CEO
Museum of Life and Science
Durham, North Carolina

Florida Reviewers

Janet M. Acerra
Forest Lakes Elementary
Oldsmar, Florida

Shannan Combee
Inwood Elementary
Winter Haven, Florida

Amber J. Cooley
Jacksonville Heights Elementary
Jacksonville, Florida

Donna de la Paz
Trinity Oaks Elementary
New Port Richey, Florida

Nancy Carrier Duncan
Eustis Heights Elementary
Eustis, Florida

Marsha Dwyer
Kenwood K-8 Center
Miami, Florida

Jessica S. Fowler
Susie E. Tolbert Elementary
Jacksonville, Florida

Pat Houston
Northwood Elementary
Crestview, Florida

Timothy W. Peterson
Romeo Elementary
Dunnellon, Florida

Rosanne Phillips
Kenwood K-8 Center
Miami, Florida

Rose M. Sedely
Eustis Heights Elementary
Eustis, Florida

Gerilyn Stark-Jerry
Chain of Lakes Elementary
Winter Haven, Florida

Deborah S. Street
Southport Elementary
Southport, Florida

Janine Townsley
Norwood Elementary
Miami, Florida

Jessica Weiss
Westchase Elementary
Tampa, Florida

Power up with Science Fusion!

Your program fuses. . .

Online Virtual Experiences

Hands-on Explorations

Active Reading

. . .to generate science energy for you.

Active Reading

Be an active reader and make this book your own!

Write your ideas, answer questions, make notes, and record activity results right on these pages.

Your book will become a record of everything you learn in science.

Hands-on Explorations

Science is all about doing.

How Are Plants of the Same Kind Different?

Observe plants to compare and contrast them. How are plants of the same kind different?

Materials
bunch of carrots

1. Observe the carrots to see how they are different. **Caution!** Do not eat the carrots.

2. Draw and write your observations.

3. Compare your drawings. How can carrots be different from one another?

Do the exciting activities on the Inquiry Flipchart.

Ask questions and test your ideas.

Draw conclusions and share what you learn.

Online Virtual Experiences

Use a computer to make science come alive.

The Cycle of Life

Quick Fact
When polar bear cubs are first born, they are blind and toothless!

Explore cool labs and activities in the virtual world.

Science Fusion
is new energy just for YOU!

Contents

THE NATURE OF SCIENCE

Unit 1—How Scientists Work 1

Big Idea 1 *The Practice of Science*

LESSON 1 What Are Senses and Other Tools? 3

LESSON 2 How Can We Use Our Senses? 15
Inquiry

LESSON 3 What Are Inquiry Skills? 17

LESSON 4 How Do We Use Inquiry Skills? 27
Inquiry

LESSON 5 How Do Scientists Work? 29

People in Science—Mary Anderson 39

Unit 1 Benchmark Review 41

EARTH AND SPACE SCIENCE

Unit 2—Objects in the Sky 43

Big Idea 5 *Earth in Space and Time*

LESSON 1 What Can We See in the Sky? 45

LESSON 2 How Do Magnifiers Work? 55
Inquiry

LESSON 3 What Does the Sun Do? 57

LESSON 4 What Is Gravity? 69

People in Science—Galileo Galilei 77

Unit 2 Benchmark Review 79

Track Your Progress

EARTH AND SPACE SCIENCE

Unit 3—Earth's Resources

Unit 3—Earth's Resources 81

Big Idea 6   *Earth Structures*

LESSON 1 **What Can We Find on Earth?** 83

LESSON 2 **What Can We Observe About Rocks?** 93
Inquiry

LESSON 3 **Where Can We Find Water?** 95

LESSON 4 **What Changes Earth?** 107

People in Science—June Bacon-Bercey 117

Unit 3 Benchmark Review 119

PHYSICAL SCIENCE

Unit 4—Matter 121

Big Idea 8   *Properties of Matter*

LESSON 1 What Can We Observe About Objects? 123

LESSON 2 Which Objects Sink or Float? 135
Inquiry

LESSON 3 How Can We Measure Temperature? 137
Inquiry

Careers in Science—Polymer Scientist 139

Unit 4 Benchmark Review 141

Unit 5—Motion 143

Big Idea 12   *Motion of Objects*

Big Idea 13   *Forces and Changes in Motion*

LESSON 1 How Do Objects Move? 145

LESSON 2 How Can We Move a Ball? 153
Inquiry

LESSON 3 How Can We Change the Way Objects Move? 155

LESSON 4 How Can We Change Motion? 167
Inquiry

People in Science—Isaac Newton 169

Unit 5 Benchmark Review 171

LIFE SCIENCE

Unit 6—Living Things............................ 173

Big Idea 14 *Organization and Development of Living Organisms*

LESSON 1 What Are Living and Nonliving Things?.............. 175

LESSON 2 How Are Plants Different?......................... 185

LESSON 3 How Are Animals Different? 195

LESSON 4 **Inquiry** What Can Your Senses Tell You About Living Things?...207

LESSON 5 What Are Some Parts of Plants?.................... 209

People in Science—Lue Gim Gong 219

Unit 6 Benchmark Review 221

LIFE SCIENCE

Unit 7—Living Things and Their Parents 223

Big Idea 16 *Heredity and Reproduction*

LESSON 1 Which Living Things Look Like Their Parents? 225

Careers in Science—Zoo Keeper 235

LESSON 2 How Are Plants of the Same Kind Different? 237
Inquiry

Unit 7 Benchmark Review 239

Unit 8—Plant and Animal Needs 241

Big Idea 17 *Interdependence*

LESSON 1 What Do Plants Need? 243

LESSON 2 Why Do Plants Grow? 253
Inquiry

People in Science—Norma Alcantar 255

LESSON 3 What Do Animals Need? 257

Unit 8 Benchmark Review 269

Interactive Glossary R1

Index. R13

How Scientists Work

© Houghton Mifflin Harcourt Publishing Company (bkgd) ©Jeff Greenberg/Alamy (inset) ©Jeff Greenberg/Alamy (border) ©Noise/Age Fotostock

Big Idea 1

The Practice of Science

Museum of Science and Industry, Tampa, Florida

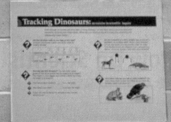

I Wonder Why
Scientists study dinosaurs. Why?
Turn the page to find out.

Here's Why Scientists study dinosaurs to learn about animals that lived long ago.

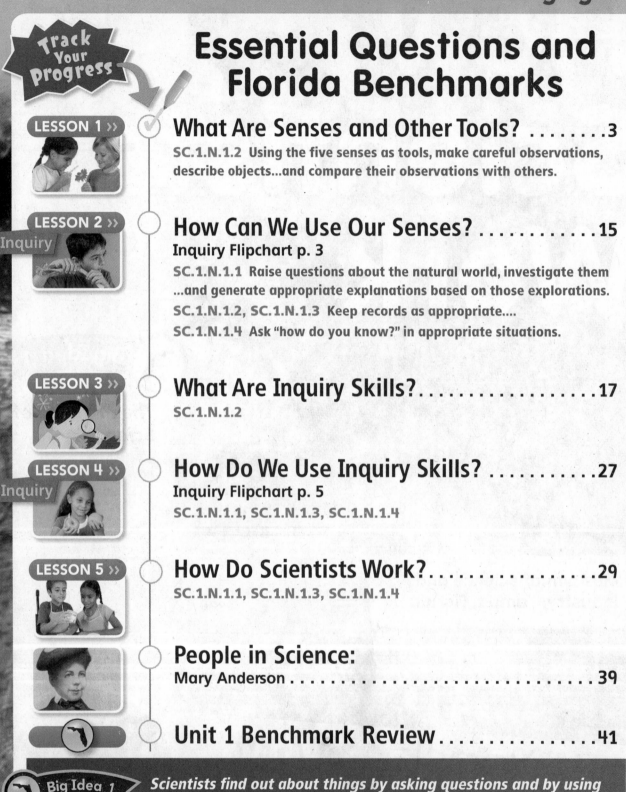

Track Your Progress

Essential Questions and Florida Benchmarks

LESSON 1 ›› What Are Senses and Other Tools? 3
SC.1.N.1.2 Using the five senses as tools, make careful observations, describe objects...and compare their observations with others.

LESSON 2 ›› How Can We Use Our Senses? 15
Inquiry
Inquiry Flipchart p. 3
SC.1.N.1.1 Raise questions about the natural world, investigate them ...and generate appropriate explanations based on those explorations.
SC.1.N.1.2, SC.1.N.1.3 Keep records as appropriate....
SC.1.N.1.4 Ask "how do you know?" in appropriate situations.

LESSON 3 ›› What Are Inquiry Skills? 17
SC.1.N.1.2

LESSON 4 ›› How Do We Use Inquiry Skills? 27
Inquiry
Inquiry Flipchart p. 5
SC.1.N.1.1, SC.1.N.1.3, SC.1.N.1.4

LESSON 5 ›› How Do Scientists Work? 29
SC.1.N.1.1, SC.1.N.1.3, SC.1.N.1.4

People in Science:
Mary Anderson 39

Unit 1 Benchmark Review 41

Big Idea 1 *Scientists find out about things by asking questions and by using the five senses to do investigations.*

Now I Get the Big Idea!

SC.1.N.1.2 Using the five senses as tools, make careful observations, describe objects in terms of number . . . and compare their observations with others.

Lesson **1**

Essential Question

What Are Senses and Other Tools?

Engage Your Brain!

Find the answer to the question in the lesson.

What sense is this child trying <u>not</u> to use?

the sense of

_____

Active Reading

Lesson Vocabulary

1 Preview the lesson.

2 Write the 2 vocabulary terms here.

_____   _____

Your Senses

How do you learn about things? You use your five senses. Your **senses** are the way you learn about the world. The senses are sight, hearing, smell, taste, and touch. You use different body parts for different senses.

Active Reading

The main idea is the most important idea about something. Draw two lines under the main idea.

You hear with your ears.

Learning with Your Senses

How can your senses help you learn?
Look at the pictures. What would your
senses tell you about each thing?

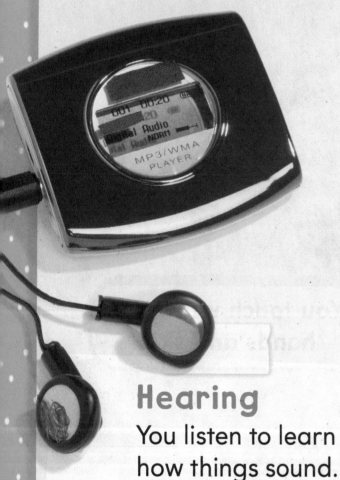

Hearing
You listen to learn
how things sound.

Touching
You touch to learn about
texture—how things feel.

▶ **Underline how you learn
how things feel.**

Seeing

You use sight to observe color, shape, and size.

Smelling

You use smell to learn how things smell.

Tasting

You taste to learn if foods are sweet, sour, or salty.

▶ **You use sight to observe three things. Circle the words.**

Tools to Explore

You can use science tools to learn more. People use **science tools** to find out about things.

A hand lens is a science tool. It helps you see small things. You could not see these things as well with just your eyes.

These children are using a hand lens to closely observe a flower.

8

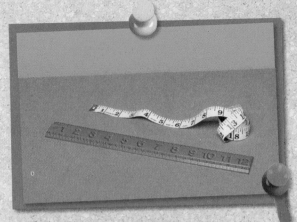

Ruler and Tape Measure

A ruler measures how long things are. A tape measure measures around things.

Measuring Cup

A measuring cup measures liquids.

Tools for Measuring

▶ Circle the names of tools you use to measure.

Balance

A balance compares how heavy things are.

Thermometer

A thermometer measures temperature. It tells how hot and cold things are.

Measuring Up

Why should we use science tools to measure? What would happen if we used different things to measure the same object? We might get different measurements.

This girl is using her shoes to measure the rug.

Do the Math!

Measure Length

Measure how long a bookcase is. Use a small shoe, a large shoe, and a tape measure or a ruler. The tape measure or ruler measures in feet.

How long is the bookcase when you measure

1. with a small shoe?

   about _____ small shoes long

2. with a big shoe?

   about _____ big shoes long

3. with a ruler or tape measure?

   about _____ feet long

Why should you use a ruler or a tape measure to measure the bookcase?

_____

_____

_____

_____

Sum It Up!

① Choose It!

Which tool is <u>not</u> used to measure? Mark an X on it.

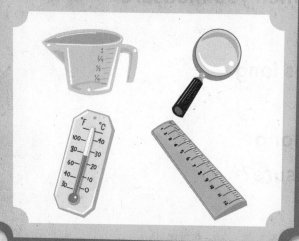

② Circle It!

Which tool helps you observe small things? Circle it.

③ Match It!

Look at each thing. Which sense helps you learn about it? Draw lines to match them.

You touch to feel how furry something is.

You see to read.

You smell food baking.

SC.1.N.1.1 Raise questions . . . investigate them in teams . . . and generate appropriate explanations based on those explorations. **SC.1.N.1.2** Using the five senses . . . make careful observations, describe objects in terms of number . . . and compare their observations with others. **SC.1.N.1.3** Keep records as appropriate . . . . **SC.1.N.1.4** Ask "how do you know?" . . . .

Name _____

Essential Question

How Can We Use Our Senses?

Set a Purpose

Tell what you want to find out.

_____

Think About the Procedure

❶ What will you observe?

_____

_____

❷ How will you find out the sound of breaking celery?

_____

Record Your Data

In this chart, record what you observe.

Sense	Observation
Sight	
Touch	
Smell	
Hear	
Taste	

Draw Conclusions

What did you find out about celery? How do you know?

_____

_____

Ask More Questions

What other questions could you ask about celery and your senses?

_____

_____

16

Essential Question

What Are Inquiry Skills?

Engage Your Brain!

Find the answer to the question in the lesson.

What can you infer this boy is doing?

The boy is

_____ .

Active Reading

Lesson Vocabulary

1 Preview the lesson.

2 Write the vocabulary term here.

_____

Skills to Help You Learn

Observe and Compare

How can you be like a scientist? You can use inquiry skills. **Inquiry skills** help you find out information. They help you learn about your world.

Active Reading

You can compare things. You find ways they are alike. A child on this page is comparing two things. Draw a triangle around the two things.

Falling Leaves Forest

observe

compare

Predict and Measure

Classify and Communicate

classify

▶ Complete the graph. How many brown birds are there?

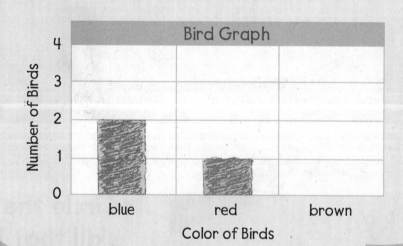

communicate

Hypothesize and Plan an Investigation

A big log rolls farther than a small log because it is heavier.

I will roll both logs down the hill to test the hypothesis.

hypothesize

plan an investigation

Rolling Logs Hill

▶ Which child made a hypothesis? Draw a line under the hypothesis.

Infer and Draw Conclusions

I think the light container is empty.

infer

Picnic Palace

Empty containers are lighter than full containers.

draw conclusions

▶ Underline the conclusion the child drew.

Make a Model and Sequence

Butterfly Garden

▶ Things may happen in order.
Write 1 beside what happens first.
Write 2 beside what happens second.
Write 3 beside what happens third.
Write 4 beside what happens last.

make a model

sequence

Sum It Up!

① Circle It!

You want to learn about something. Circle what you do to find out.

predict

classify

plan an investigation

② Choose It!

What inquiry skill does this show?

communicate

make a model

sequence

③ Draw It!

Observe an object. Draw it. Tell about it.

This is a _____. It is _____.

Name _____

Word Play

Circle the letters to spell the words.
Then complete the sentence.

compare	classify	infer	measure
observe	predict	sequence	

```
s e q u e n c e a a
v c l a s s i f y
u l r i n f e r t
r m e a s u r e p
o b s e r v e g e
e w p r e d i c t
c o m p a r e t z
```

All the words in the puzzle
are _____ .

Apply Concepts

Circle the word that matches the meaning.

1 tell what you learn	communicate	observe
2 sort things into groups	sequence	classify
3 tell how things are alike and different	make a model	compare
4 put things in order	sequence	hypothesize
5 find out how much or how long	measure	infer
6 use your senses	make a model	observe
7 make a good guess about what will happen	predict	sequence
8 decide what steps to follow	draw conclusions	plan an investigation

Take It Home!

Family Members: Discuss with your child how inquiry skills are used around the home. For example, you measure when you cook and classify when you sort laundry.

26

SC.1.N.1.1 Raise questions . . . investigate them in teams . . . and generate appropriate explanations based on those explorations. **SC.1.N.1.3** Keep records as appropriate . . . . **SC.1.N.1.4** Ask "how do you know?" . . . .

Name _____

Essential Question

How Do We Use Inquiry Skills?

Set a Purpose

Tell what you want to find out.

_____

_____

_____

Think About the Procedure

1 What fair test did you plan? Write your plan here.

_____

_____

2 What science tools will you use for your test?

_____

Record Your Data

Draw or write. Record what you observe.

Draw Conclusions

What conclusions can you draw?

_____

_____

Ask More Questions

What other questions could you ask?

_____

_____

SC.1.N.1.1 Raise questions . . . investigate them in teams . . . and generate appropriate explanations based on those explorations.
SC.1.N.1.3 Keep records as appropriate . . . .

Essential Question

How Do Scientists Work?

Engage Your Brain!

Find the answer to the question in the lesson.

How do you paint a rainbow using only three colors of paint?

You can mix

_____.

Active Reading

Lesson Vocabulary

1 Preview the lesson.

2 Write the vocabulary term here.

_____

Think Like a Scientist

Scientists plan an investigation when they want to learn more. An **investigation** is a test scientists do. There are different plans for investigations. Here is one plan.

Observe

First, observe something. Ask a question about it.

What would happen if we mixed yellow paint and blue paint?

Hypothesize and Make a Plan

Next, make a hypothesis. State something you can test. Plan a fair test to see whether you are correct.

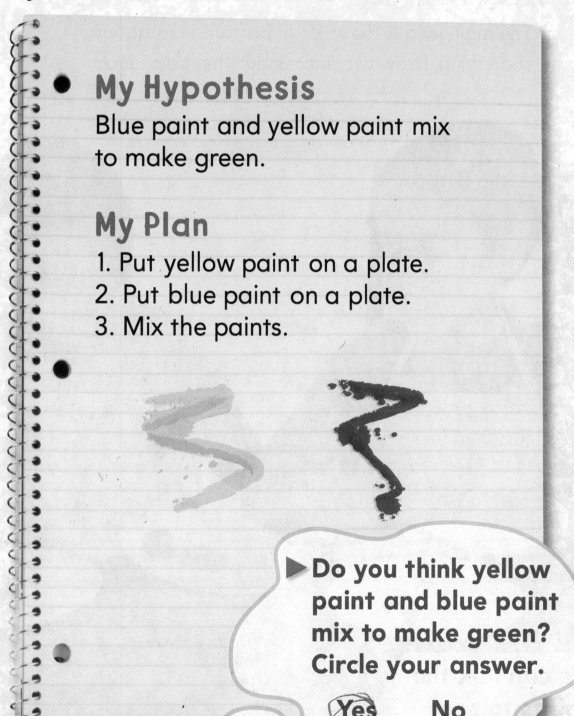

My Hypothesis

Blue paint and yellow paint mix to make green.

My Plan

1. Put yellow paint on a plate.
2. Put blue paint on a plate.
3. Mix the paints.

▶ **Do you think yellow paint and blue paint mix to make green? Circle your answer.**

Yes **No**

Do the Test

Do the test. Follow the steps of your plan. Observe what happens.

We can mix the paints to see what happens.

Draw Conclusions

Draw conclusions from your test. What did you learn? Compare your results with your classmates' results. What would happen if you did the test again? How do you know?

If we do the test again, yellow paint and blue paint will still make green.

▶ Circle the color that yellow and blue make when you mix them.

Record What You Observe

Scientists record what they learn from an investigation. You can keep a record in a science notebook. You can draw pictures. You can write.

Active Reading

A detail is a fact about a main idea. Draw one line under a detail. Draw an arrow to the main idea it tells about.

▶ **What colors make green?**

Blue and Yellow

Sum It Up!

① Write It!

You have a [feather] and a [block].
You will drop them.
You think the block will fall faster.
How can you test your idea?

_____

② Circle It!

You do the steps in an investigation.
Now you draw what happens.
Which step are you doing?
Circle it.

Observe.   Plan a fair test.

Record what you observe.

 **Brain Check**

Lesson 5

Name _____

Word Play

Unscramble the word to complete each sentence. Use these words if you need help.

observe	hypothesize	investigation	record

ntiovetigansi

① To learn more about something, you do an _____.

eyhtpoheszi

② When you make a statement you can test, you _____.

dreorc

③ After you do a test, you should _____ your results.

beosver

④ When you look at something closely, you _____ it.

37

Apply Concepts

Can air move a penny and a feather?
Tell how you could investigate.
Write a number from 1 to 5 to show the order.

_____ Write a plan.

_____ Ask a question–
Can air move a penny and a feather?

_____ Record what you observe.

_____ Share your results.

_____ Follow your plan.

38

Learn About...
Mary Anderson

In 1902, Mary Anderson observed something. In bad weather, drivers had trouble seeing. They had to drive with the window open. Or they had to get out to clean off the windshield. Anderson got an idea. She invented the windshield wiper.

Drivers could use it from inside their vehicle. They could see the road and stay warm and dry.

Fun Fact

By the 1920s all cars had windshield wipers.

This Leads to That

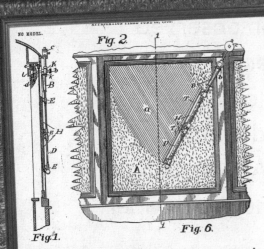

Mary Anderson invented the first windshield wiper. This shows an early drawing.

Robert Kearns invented a windshield wiper that went on and off as needed.

▶ **How does Mary Anderson's invention help people today?**

_____

_____

_____

_____

Multiple Choice

Fill in the circle next to the best answer.

SC.1.N.1.2

① What can the children learn from listening to the music?

Ⓐ how it feels

Ⓑ how it looks

Ⓒ how it sounds

SC.1.N.1.2

② You observe the plants. You think about what you know. You use these things to decide what something means. What are you doing?

Ⓐ classifying the plants

Ⓑ drawing a conclusion

Ⓒ predicting what will happen

SC.1.N.1.1

3 What step in a science inquiry is shown here?

Ⓐ comparing results

Ⓑ doing a test

Ⓒ observing

SC.1.N.1.2

4 Which sentence compares the lemon and the banana?

Ⓐ The banana has a soft inside.

Ⓑ The lemon is very sour.

Ⓒ Both fruits are yellow.

SC.1.N.1.3

5 You investigate to find out whether soil or sand holds more water. What can you do to record what you observe?

Ⓐ Draw a picture.

Ⓑ Tell a friend.

Ⓒ Think about it.

SC.1.N.1.4

6 How do you know an apple is larger than a grape?

Ⓐ You measure them.

Ⓑ You sort them.

Ⓒ You taste them.

Objects in the Sky

Big Idea 5

Earth in Space and Time

I Wonder Why

Large objects in the sky look very small. Why?

Turn the page to find out.

UNIT 2

Here's Why Large objects in the sky look small because they are far away.

Track Your Progress

Essential Questions and Florida Benchmarks

 **LESSON 1 »**

What Can We See in the Sky? 45

SC.1.E.5.1 Observe and discuss that there are more stars in the sky than anyone can easily count and that they are not scattered evenly in the sky.
SC.1.E.5.3 Investigate how magnifiers make things appear bigger and help people see things they could not see without them.

 **LESSON 2 »**
Inquiry

How Do Magnifiers Work? 55

Inquiry Flipchart p. 8
SC.1.E.5.3 Investigate how magnifiers make things appear bigger and help people see things they could not see without them.
SC.1.N.1.1, SC.1.N.1.2, SC.1.N.1.3

 **LESSON 3 »**

What Does the Sun Do? 57

SC.1.E.5.4 Identify the beneficial and harmful properties of the Sun.

 **LESSON 4 »**

What Is Gravity? 69

SC.1.E.5.2 Explore the Law of Gravity by demonstrating that Earth's gravity pulls any object on or near Earth toward it even though nothing is touching the object.

People in Science:
Galileo Galilei 77

Unit 2 Benchmark Review 79

 **Big Idea 5** *People explore space to learn more about Earth and our solar system. Gravity and energy help form galaxies, stars, the solar system, and Earth.*

Now I Get the Big Idea!

44

Essential Question

What Can We See in the Sky?

Engage Your Brain!

Find the answer to the question in the lesson.

When can you see the moon?

_____

Active Reading

Lesson Vocabulary

1 Preview the lesson.

2 Write the 5 vocabulary terms here.

_____   _____

_____   _____

_____

Good Morning, Sunshine

sun

Look up! You can see many things in the daytime sky. You can see the sun. The **sun** is the star closest to Earth. A **star** is an object in the sky. It gives off its own light. The sun gives light and heat to Earth.

You may also see clouds in the daytime sky. Sometimes, you can even see the moon.

Active Reading

The main idea is the most important idea about something. Draw two lines under the main idea.

clouds

► **What can you see in the daytime sky? Look out your window. Draw what you see.**

Good Night, Sky

moon

You can see many things in the nighttime sky. You may see the moon. The **moon** is a large sphere, or ball of rock. It does not give off its own light. You may also see clouds at night.

Active Reading

Draw one line under a detail. Draw an arrow to the main idea it tells about.

You may see stars in the nighttime sky. There are too many stars to count. They are not evenly spaced in the sky.

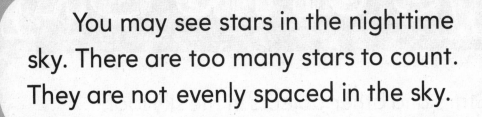

star

Do the Math!

Compare Solid Shapes

Many objects in the sky are spheres. A sphere is a round ball. The moon is a sphere. So is the sun. Color the spheres below.

Eye on the Sky

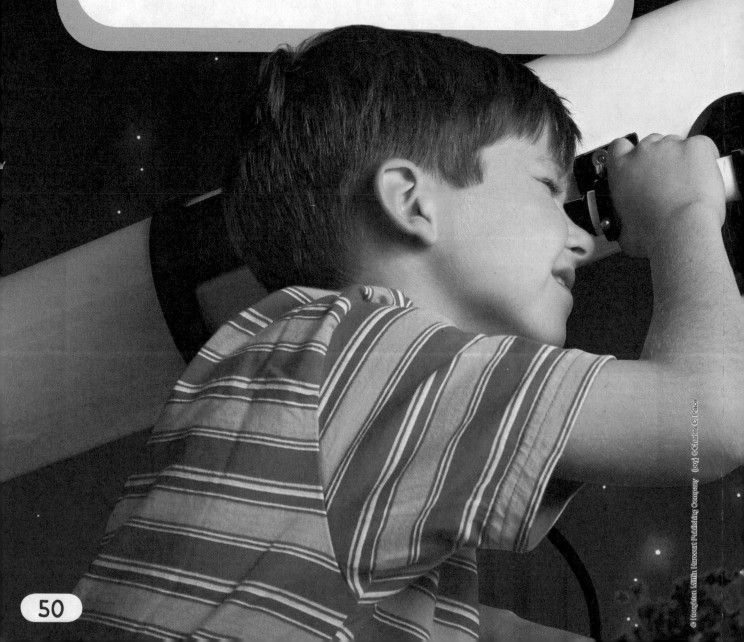

Stars and other objects in the sky look small. We can magnify them to see them better. **Magnify** means to make something look bigger. A **telescope** is a tool that helps us magnify things in the sky.

▶ **Which picture shows the moon through a telescope? Mark an X on it.**

telescope

Both pictures show the moon.

Sum It Up!

① Solve It!

Solve the riddle.

I am a tool. I make things look bigger. You can use me to observe things in the sky.

What am I?

_____

② Circle It!

Circle true or false.

Stars are evenly spaced in the sky.

true   false

Stars give off their own light.

true   false

③ Draw It!

Draw what you can see in the sky at both times.

daytime	nighttime
	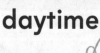

Name Maximas

Word Play

Unscramble the letters to complete each sentence.

sun | star | telescope | magnify | moon

omon   The **M o o n** is a large ball of rock.

tasr   A **S t a r** gives off its own light.

eletopsce   A **t e l e s c o p e** is a tool for making things look bigger.

usn   The **S u n** is the star we see in the day.

fimgany   To **m a g n i f y** is to make things look bigger.

Apply Concepts

1 Fill in the diagram to compare.
Use the words below.

sun	stars	clouds	moon

daytime
sky   both   nighttime
sky

2 Draw a nighttime sky full of stars.

Take It Home!

Family Members: Observe the nighttime sky with your child. Have your child explain how it looks different from the daytime sky.

SC.1.N.1.1 Raise questions ... investigate them in teams ... and generate appropriate explanations based on those explorations. **SC.1.N.1.2** Using the five senses ... make careful observations, describe objects in terms of number ... and compare their observations with others. **SC.1.N.1.3** Keep records as appropriate ... **SC.1.E.5.3** Investigate how magnifiers make things appear bigger ....

Name _____

Essential Question

How Do Magnifiers Work?

Set a Purpose

Tell what you want to find out.

_____

_____

Think About the Procedure

❶ Why do you use a hand lens to magnify things?

_____

❷ Why do you need to compare your drawings?

_____

_____

_____

Record Your Data

Draw to record what you observe.

Observations	
salt without a hand lens	
salt with a hand lens	

Draw Conclusions

How can a hand lens help you observe?

_____

_____

Ask More Questions

What other questions could you answer by observing with a magnifier?

_____

_____

SC.1.E.5.4 Identify the beneficial and harmful properties of the Sun.

Essential Question

What Does the Sun Do?

Engage Your Brain!

Find the answer to the question in the lesson.

What would Earth be like without the sun?

_____

Active Reading

Lesson Vocabulary

1 Preview the lesson.

2 Write the 3 vocabulary terms here.

_____   _____

_____

© Houghton Mifflin Harcourt Publishing Company (bkgd) ©BRUCE COLEMAN INC./Alamy

We Need the Sun

Lighting the Way

We get different kinds of energy from the sun. **Energy** is something that causes matter to move or change.

Light is energy that lets us see. We use light from the sun to read and play. Plants use light from the sun to grow.

Active Reading

Find the sentence that tells what energy is. Draw a line under the sentence.

Warming It Up

Heat is energy that makes things warmer. The sun makes its own heat. The heat from the sun warms land, air, and water on Earth. The sun's heat makes Earth warm enough for living things.

▶ **An animal is getting heat. Circle it.**

Watch Out!

Light and heat from the sun can also be harmful. Light can burn our skin. It can hurt our eyes. It can cause some things to fade. Heat can cause some things to melt.

Active Reading

The main idea is the most important idea about something. Draw two lines under the main idea.

new slide

slide faded by the sun

melting ice cream

melting crayons

▶ **What is making the crayons and ice cream melt? Circle it.**

Sun Safety

You can stay safe in the sun. Follow the rules below!

Staying Safe in the Sun

1 Wear sunscreen.

2 Wear clothes that cover your skin.

3 Wear a hat to protect your face.

4 Wear sunglasses to protect your eyes.

5 Use an umbrella for shade.

6 Drink a lot of water.

▶ Some people are not staying safe in the sun. Cut out the pictures from the end of the lesson. Use them to show how the people can stay safe.

Sum It Up!

① Solve It!

Solve the riddle.

I give light to help you see.

Earth is warm, thanks to me.

My energy helps plants grow.

I'm the closest star you know!

What am I?

_____

② Circle It!

Which things help you stay safe from the sun? Circle them.

Brain Check

Name ______________________

Word Play

Use these words to complete the puzzle.

sunscreen heat light energy sun

Across

1. the star that gives light and heat to Earth
2. energy that keeps Earth warm
3. light and heat

Down

1. something we wear to protect our skin from the sun
4. energy that helps us see

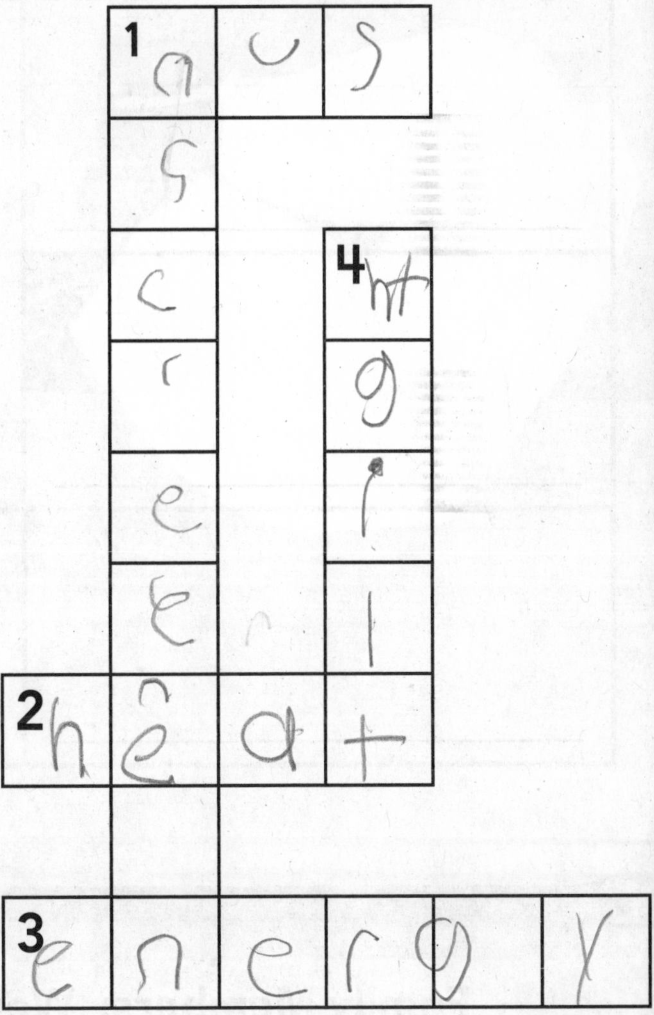

Fill in the chart.

How is the sun helpful and harmful?

Helpful	Harmful
gives heat	can burn skin

Family Members: Work with your child to identify items in your home that help your family stay safe from the sun.

Take It Home!

Essential Question

What Is Gravity?

Engage Your Brain!

Find the answer to the question in the lesson.

What is pulling the diver down?

gravity?

Active Reading

Lesson Vocabulary

1 Preview the lesson.

2 Write the vocabulary term here.

_____

What Goes Up

Must Come Down

Look at the boy jumping. Soon he will come back down to the ground. Why doesn't he float away? It is because of gravity. **Gravity** pulls things down to Earth.

Active Reading

Clue words can help you find a cause. **Because** is a clue word. Draw a box around **because**.

Gravity pulls things down unless something holds them up. The bed holds one girl up off the floor. Gravity pulls the bear down without touching it.

▶ **Where will the teddy bear go? Draw an arrow to show its path.**

Sports Fun

Did you know that you use gravity to play sports? You push against gravity every time you move your body or throw something. Pushing against gravity is hard to do.

Soon gravity will pull the ball back down.

The girl pushes against gravity as she throws the ball.

► **How does the girl use her body to push?**

She Usees
her hands a feets

The girl pushes against gravity to jump.

Do the Math!

Solve a Problem

Lee did 3 pull-ups every day for 3 days. How many did he do in all? Use the number line to skip-count.

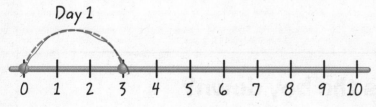

Day 1

0 1 2 3 4 5 6 7 8 9 10

_____ **pull-ups**

Sum It Up!

1 Think About It!

Look at the first picture. What happens next? Draw to show where the boy goes.

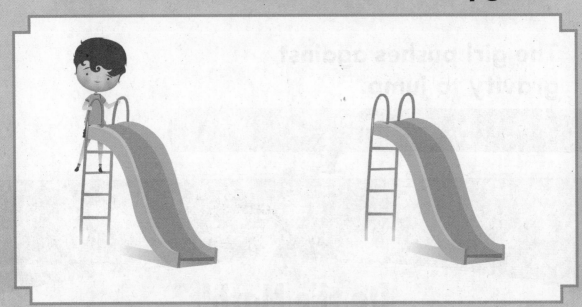

2 Write It!

Look at the boy you drew above. What holds him off the ground?

_____

What pulls the boy down?

_____

 **Brain Check**

Name _____

Word Play

Use these words to fill in the blanks.
Then find each word in the puzzle.

gravity	pull	up	down	fall

1. If you drop a ball, it falls _down_.

2. A chair holds you _up_ off the ground.

3. You push against _Gravity_ when you lift a ball.

4. A book will _fall_ if nothing holds it up.

5. Gravity can _Pull_ things to Earth.

```
p  u  l  l  r  g  u
b  e  f  e  r  g  p
g  r  a  v  i  t  y
y  e  l  e  d  g  j
o  m  l  t  o  z  v
k  f  u  b  w  w  r
g  n  y  i  n  d  a
```

Apply Concepts

Fill in the web with facts about gravity.

down   Earth   holds   push

Gravity pulls things down to _____ .

You _____ against gravity when you jump.

gravity

An object falls unless something _____ it up.

Gravity pulls objects _____ without touching them.

Take It Home!

Family Members: Have your child name his or her favorite sport and explain how he or she pushes against gravity to play it.

4 Things to Know About Galileo Galilei

1 Galileo lived in Italy more than 400 years ago.

2 His telescope made objects look 20 times bigger.

3 He discovered sunspots on the sun.

4 He found out that the planet Jupiter has four moons.

This Leads to That

Galileo used his telescope to observe the sun and planets.

He proved that Earth moves around the sun.

▶ **People used to think that the sun moved around Earth. Galileo proved this was wrong. Why is this important?**

_____

_____

_____

UNIT 3
Earth's Resources

Big Idea 6

Earth Structures

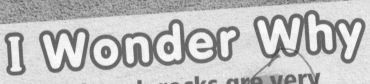

footprints on a Florida beach

I Wonder Why
Some beach rocks are very smooth. Why?
Turn the page to find out.

Here's Why Water from the ocean wears down the rocks. The rocks rub together and become smooth over time.

Track Your Progress

Essential Questions and Florida Benchmarks

LESSON 1 »

What Can We Find on Earth? 83
SC.1.E.6.1 Recognize that water, rocks, soil, and living organisms are found on Earth's surface.
SC.1.E.6.2 Describe the need for water and how to be safe around water.

LESSON 2 »

Inquiry

What Can We Observe About Rocks? 93
Inquiry Flipchart p. 12
SC.1.E.6.1 Recognize that water, rocks, soil, and living organisms are found on Earth's surface.
SC.1.N.1.1, SC.1.N.1.2, SC.1.N.1.3

LESSON 3 »

Where Can We Find Water? 95
SC.1.E.6.1, SC.1.E.6.2

LESSON 4 »

What Changes Earth? 107
SC.1.E.6.3 Recognize that some things in the world around us happen fast and some happen slowly.

People in Science:
June Bacon-Bercey. 117

Unit 3 Benchmark Review 119

Big Idea 6 *Earth and its surface are made up of many things. Changes can occur to Earth's surface. Living things need resources from Earth.*

Now I Get the Big Idea!

Essential Question

What Can We Find on Earth?

🧠 Engage Your Brain!

Find the answer in the lesson.

The Great Sphinx was built long ago.

It was built from

_____.

Active Reading

Lesson Vocabulary

1 Preview the lesson.

2 Write the 3 vocabulary terms here.

_____   _____

_____

All Natural

What do you use from Earth? You use natural resources. A **natural resource** is anything from nature that people can use.

Air

Air is a natural resource. We breathe air. Wind is moving air. This hang glider uses wind to move. A wind farm changes wind into useful energy. Energy gives light and heat to homes.

Active Reading

Draw two lines under the main idea.

Water

Water is a natural resource.
We use water in many ways.

▶ **Label each picture. Tell how people use water.**

ShI am vash the Dog

I am DancK

I AM givin My Ship

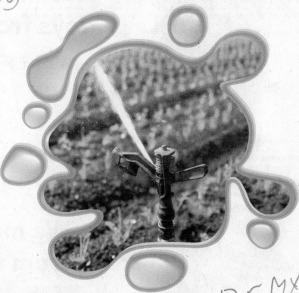

I am waDr MXPlos

Plants and Animals

Plants and animals are natural resources too. We use them for food. We also use them to make clothes and other things we need.

▶ **Look at the pictures. Circle the good we get from each plant or animal.**

We make socks from cotton.

We make wood toys from trees.

We make food from tomatoes.

We make a sweater from a sheep's wool.

We make cheese from a cow's milk.

We get eggs from a hen.

Rocks

Rocks are a natural resource. A **rock** is a hard nonliving object from the ground. We use rocks to build things.

Active Reading

Find the sentence that tells the meaning of **rock**. Draw a line under the sentence.

house made from rocks

Soil

Soil is a natural resource, too. **Soil** is the top layer of Earth. We use soil to grow plants. We can also use it to make things. We can use bricks for building.

▶ **How is this boy using soil?**

_____

_____

① Write It!

Solve the riddle.

How are a , , and a alike?

They are all _nacher_.

② Circle It!

Circle a way people use each natural resource.

Animal	Rock	Water	Soil

Name _____

Word Play

Write the resources on the lines.
Then color the picture.

~~App~~ Apple

1. What fruit comes from a plant? _Apple_____
   Color it red.

2. What other resources are plants? _Cow_____
   Color them green.

3. What resource is an animal? _grass_____
   Color it brown.

4. What resource do we drink? _Water_____
   Color it blue.

Apply Concepts

Fill in the organizer. Write the names of natural resources.

air   plants

water   rocks

soil   animal

Natural Resources

Take It Home!

Family Members: Work with your child to identify things in your home that are made from natural resources.

Name _____

SC.1.N.1.1 Raise questions ... investigate them in teams ... and generate appropriate explanations based on those explorations. **SC.1.N.1.2** Using the five senses ... make careful observations, describe objects in terms of number ... and compare their observations with others. **SC.1.N.1.3** Keep records as appropriate .... **SC.1.E.6.1** Recognize that ... rocks ... are found on Earth's surface.

Essential Question

What Can We Observe About Rocks?

Set a Purpose
Tell what you want to find out.

_____

_____

Think About the Procedure
❶ What do you find out when you observe the rocks?

_____

_____

❷ What are some ways you can sort rocks?

_____

Record Your Data

Draw or write about how you sorted the rocks.

Ways I Sorted		

Draw Conclusions

How can rocks be alike and different?

_____

_____

_____

Ask More Questions

What other things about rocks could you test?

_____

_____

94

SC.1.E.6.1 Recognize that water ... found on Earth's surface.
SC.1.E.6.2 Describe the need for water and how to be safe around water.

Essential Question

Where Can We Find Water?

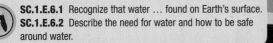

Engage Your Brain!

Find the answer to the question in the lesson.

How much of Earth is covered with water?

_____

Active Reading

Lesson Vocabulary

1 Preview the lesson.

2 Write the 4 vocabulary terms here.

_____   _____

_____   _____

95

So Fresh

Most plants and animals need fresh water. People need fresh water too. Fresh water is not salty. You can find fresh water in many places.

Streams

A **stream** is a small body of flowing water.

Rivers

Some streams flow into rivers. A **river** is a large body of flowing water.

_____

_____

Lakes

A **lake** is a body of water with land all around it. Water in a lake does not flow.

So Salty

You can find water in oceans too. An **ocean** is a large body of salty water. Most of Earth's water is in oceans.

Active Reading

A detail is a fact about a main idea. Draw one line under a detail. Draw an arrow to the main idea it tells about.

surfer in ocean

About $\frac{3}{4}$, or three fourths, of Earth is covered with water. The rest is covered with land.

This circle models Earth's water and land. It has 4 parts. Color the parts to show how much water is on Earth.

Now look at the circle. How much of Earth is covered with land?

Answer: _____

Wonderful Water

All living things need water. Plants, animals, and people need it to stay healthy.

Active Reading

The main idea is the most important idea about something. Draw two lines under the main idea.

People drink water.

Animals drink water.

Save Earth's water!

Water flows through this dam.

We must protect water and keep it clean.

Follow these tips to help.

1. Use less water for baths and showers.

2. Fix leaky pipes or faucets.

3. Put trash in trash cans! Do not put trash in water.

▶ **Add your own tip for protecting Earth's water.**

_____

_____

_____

Plants need water too.

Jump into Safety!

Water Safety

- Learn to swim.
- Never swim alone.
- Watch the weather.
- Wear a life jacket on a boat.
- Do not dive in shallow water.
- Call 911 if there is an emergency.

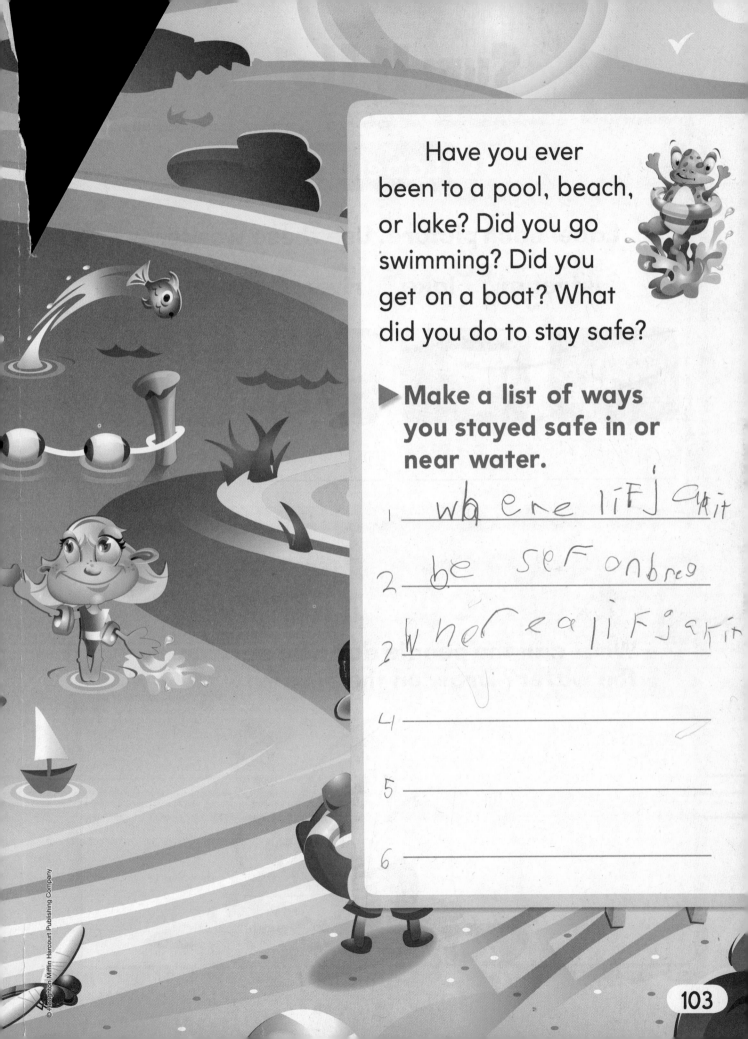

Have you ever been to a pool, beach, or lake? Did you go swimming? Did you get on a boat? What did you do to stay safe?

▶ **Make a list of ways you stayed safe in or near water.**

1. wa ene liFj ayit
2. be seF anbres
3. wher e a li Fj ak in
4.
5.
6.

Sum It Up!

① Label It!

Label each picture. Use these words.

stream   lake   river   ocean

river   lake   ocean   stream

② Draw It!

What can the people do to be safe on the water? Draw on the picture.

Name _____

Word Play

Fill in the blanks. Use these words.

| ocean | lake | stream | river | fresh water |

Most lakes have _f r e s h (w) a t e r_ .

An _o c e (a) n_ has salty water.

A _s (t) r e a m_ is a small body of water.

A _(l) a k (e)_ has water that does not flow.

Streams can flow together to
make a _(r) i v e r_ .

**Then use the circled letters
to fill in the blanks below.**
We use _W a t e r_ in
many ways!

Apply Concepts

Write your answer to each question.

1 **Why do we need water?**

we xed watere
whel;f gack
bo'nat runBiytne pa

2 **How can we stay safe around water?**

- _____

- _____

- _____

- _____

Take It Home!

Family Members: Work with your child to identify ways to save water at home.

106

SC.1.E.6.3 Recognize that some things in the world around us happen fast and some happen slowly.

Lesson **4**

Essential Question

What Changes Earth?

Engage Your Brain!

Find the answer to the question in the lesson.

What changed the shape of these rocks over time?

_____

Active Reading

Lesson Vocabulary

1 Preview the lesson.

2 Write the 6 vocabulary terms here.

Flood   erosion

volcano   drought

wethering   earthquake

Make It Fast

Earth is always changing. Some changes are fast. They happen in minutes, hours, or days.

An earthquake is a fast change. An **earthquake** is a shaking of Earth's surface. Floods and eruptions from volcanoes are fast changes too. A **volcano** is a place where hot melted rock comes out of the ground.

earthquake

Active Reading

An effect tells what happens. Draw two lines under an effect.

A **flood** happens when streams, rivers, or lakes get too full.

flood

volcano erupting

▶ **Circle the labels that name fast changes.**

Take It Slow

Some changes to Earth are slow. Slow changes happen over many months or years. Weathering is a slow change. **Weathering** happens when wind and water break down rock into smaller pieces. Erosion is also a slow change. **Erosion** happens when wind and water move rocks and soil. It changes the shape of land.

Active Reading

Draw one line under a detail. Draw an arrow to the main idea it tells about.

Erosion wears away the cliff.

drought

A drought is another slow change. A **drought** is a long time with very little rain. The land gets very dry.

▶ Can a drought last for minutes or for years?

yo ora xers

Weathering and erosion have worn down these rocks.

Make a Match

Look at the **Before** and **After** pictures. Make three matches.

▶ Write the number of a **Before** picture on the **After** picture that matches.

Before

1

wall arch

2

land

3

Mount Saint Helens

1 weathering

3 volcano

2 flood

Sum It Up!

① Circle It!

Look at each picture. Then circle the effect.

Trees dry out.
Trees are burned.

Land is covered with water.
Land gets dry.

② Draw It!

**Draw two changes to Earth. Label each
fast or slow.**

4 Things to Know About

June Bacon-Bercey

1 June Bacon-Bercey is a meteorologist.

2 She was the first female meteorologist on television.

3 She won money, which she used to help other women become meteorologists.

4 She enjoys teaching.

Word Whiz

▶ **Learn weather words. Find the words in the word search below. Draw a circle around each word you find.**

tornado hurricane lightning thunder storm blizzard

l i g h t n i n g q
w m r n o t b y v h
b d l z r x s p c u
l t h u n d e r b r
i j g s a y z q m r
z q f g d g f d s i
z w s t o r m h j c
a r d k y y p l k a
r t s h p q w r t n
d y p f j s d c b e

Name TaylorLewis

Multiple Choice

Fill in the circle next to the best answer.

SC.1.E.6.2

1 What is one way to stay safe around water?

🔘 learn to swim

Ⓑ never throw trash in the water

Ⓒ turn off the water when you brush your teeth

SC.1.E.6.2

2 How can you use water?

Ⓐ for eating

Ⓑ for breathing

🔘 for drinking

SC.1.E.6.1

3 Which is a natural resource?

Ⓐ

Ⓑ

Ⓒ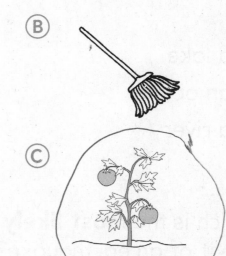

SC.1.E.6.1

4 What is this body of water?

Ⓐ a lake

Ⓑ an ocean

Ⓒ a river

SC.1.E.6.3

5 Which is the **most likely** effect of an earthquake?

Ⓐ Bridges fall down.

Ⓑ Forests grow.

Ⓒ Rivers overflow.

SC.1.E.6.1

6 What can you observe about rocks from this picture?

Ⓐ Rocks come from trees.

Ⓑ Rocks are found in and on Earth's surface.

Ⓒ Rocks can be different colors.

UNIT 4
Matter

sand castle on Florida beach

I Wonder Why
We use the words brown and rough to tell about this sand castle. Why?
Turn the page to find out.

Here's Why Brown and rough are properties of the sand castle. A property is one part of what something is like.

Track Your Progress

Essential Questions and Florida Benchmarks

LESSON 1 »

What Can We Observe About Objects?.. 123

SC.1.P.8.1 Sort objects by observable properties, such as size, shape, color, temperature (hot or cold), weight (heavy or light), texture, and whether objects sink or float.

LESSON 2 »
Inquiry

Which Objects Sink or Float?...........135

Inquiry Flipchart p. 16

SC.1.P.8.1 Sort objects by observable properties, such as size, shape, color, temperature (hot or cold), weight (heavy or light), texture, and whether objects sink or float.

SC.1.N.1.1, SC.1.N.1.3, SC.1.N.1.4

LESSON 3 »
Inquiry

How Can We Measure Temperature? 137

Inquiry Flipchart p. 17

SC.1.P.8.1 Sort objects by observable properties, such as size, shape, color, temperature (hot or cold), weight (heavy or light), texture, and whether objects sink or float.

SC.1.N.1.1, SC.1.N.1.3, SC.1.N.1.4

Careers in Science:
Polymer Scientist........................ **139**

Unit 4 Benchmark Review 141

Big Idea 8 *All objects are matter. All matter has properties. Properties are used to classify matter.*

Now I Get the Big Idea!

SC.1.P.8.1 Sort objects by observable properties, such as size, shape, color, temperature (hot or cold), weight (heavy or light), texture, and whether objects sink or float.

Essential Question

What Can We Observe About Objects?

Engage Your Brain!

Find the answer to the question in the lesson.

How are the blocks in this rabbit the same?

They are all

_____ .

Active Reading

Lesson Vocabulary

1 Preview the lesson.

2 Write the 5 vocabulary terms here.

_____   _____

_____   _____

_____

Why Matter Matters

Look around. What do you see? Are there trees, toys, or books? These things are matter. **Matter** is anything that takes up space. Even the air you breathe is matter!

▶ Look at the ball, the clock, and the boy. Draw an X on each thing that is matter.

What's It Like?

A **property** of matter is one part of what something is like. Some properties are size, shape, color, and texture. **Texture** is what an object feels like.

Active Reading

Find the sentence that tells the meaning of property. Draw a line under the sentence.

Size

Big and **small** are words that tell about size.

Shape

Star and **heart** are words that tell about shape.

▶ **In each box, draw an X on the object that does not belong.**

Color

Red and **blue** are words that tell about color.

Texture

Soft and **hard** are words that tell about texture.

Heavy or Light?

Some things you pick up feel light.
Others feel heavy. **Weight** is the measure
of how heavy an object feels.

heavy

light

Do the Math!

Order by Weight

Order from light to heavy. Write 1 for lightest.
Write 3 for heaviest.

paint

paper clip

marker

Hot or Cold?

How hot is a pizza? How cold is an ice pop? You can find out by using temperature. **Temperature** is the measure of how warm something is.

pizza

ice pop

hot cocoa

lemonade

▶ Draw something hot.

▶ Draw something cold.

Will It Sink or Will It Float?

Think about things in a tub or a pool. A sponge may stay on top of the water. A bar of soap may go to the bottom.

An object that floats stays on top of a liquid. An object that sinks falls to the bottom.

▶Circle what floats. Draw an X on what sinks.

The canoe with people is big and heavy.

Why does it float?

How Does That Boat Float?

Look at the clay boat and the clay ball. The ball sinks. The boat floats. Why? The ball and the boat have different shapes. The shape of the boat helps it float. Sometimes changing the shape of something makes it sink or float.

Sum It Up!

① Choose It!

Circle each blue shape. Draw an X on each square. Underline each big circle.

② Mark It!

Draw an X on the small dog.

③ Write It!

Is this toy soft or hard? Write the word.

_____

Name _____

Word Play

Write the word from the box for each clue.

| property | weight | texture | temperature |

the measure of how warm something is

t e (M) p e r (a) t u r e
     (1)   (2)

the way something feels

(t) e x (T) u r e
(3)   (4)

the measure of how heavy something feels

w (e) i g h t
  (5)

a part of what something is like

p r o p e (r) t y
            (6)

Solve the riddle. Write the circled letters in order on the lines below.

I am anything that takes up space. What am I?

M a T t e r
1 2 3 4 5 6

Apply Concepts

1 Sort these shapes. Draw each one in the diagram.

hearts   red

red hearts

2 Circle each thing that floats.

Draw an X on each thing that sinks.

3 Name or draw something hot. _____

Name or draw something cold. _____

Take It Home!

Family Members: Ask your child to tell you about the properties of matter. Point out an object at home. Have your child tell about the object's properties.

SC.1.N.1.1 Raise questions ... investigate them in teams ... and generate appropriate explanations based on those explorations. **SC.1.N.1.3** Keep records as appropriate .... **SC.1.N.1.4** Ask "how do you know?" .... **SC.1.P.8.1** Sort objects by observable properties ... and whether objects sink or float.

Name _____

Essential Question

Which Objects Sink or Float?

Set a Purpose

Tell what you will find out from this activity.

_____

Think About the Procedure

1 Why do you need a bowl of water?

_____

_____

2 What do you know about an object if it stays on top of the water?

_____

3 How do you know if an object sinks?

_____

Record Your Data

Record what you observe.

Float	Sink
_____	_____

Compare Observations

Compare your data with a classmate's data.
How are they the same? How are they different?

_____

_____

Draw Conclusions

Which objects float? Which objects sink?

_____

_____

Ask More Questions

What other things about sink and float can you test?

_____

© Houghton Mifflin Harcourt Publishing Company

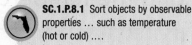

SC.1.P.8.1 Sort objects by observable properties ... such as temperature (hot or cold) ....

Name _____

Essential Question

How Can We Measure Temperature?

Set a Purpose

Tell what you will find out.

_____

_____

Think About the Procedure

❶ How will you test whether light colors or dark colors warm up faster?

_____

_____

❷ How do you know which color warms up faster?

_____

_____

Record Your Data

In this chart, record the temperature at the beginning and the temperature after 30 minutes.

Color	Beginning Temperature	Temperature After 30 Minutes
White		
Black		

Draw Conclusions

Do light colors or dark colors warm up faster?

_____

Ask More Questions

What other questions about temperature could you test and measure?

_____

_____

_____

SC.1.P.8.1 Sort objects by observable properties, such as size, shape, color, temperature (hot or cold), weight (heavy or light), texture, and whether objects sink or float.

Ask a Polymer Scientist

What are polymers?

Polymers are a kind of material. We can find some polymers, such as silk, in nature. Scientists make other polymers, such as plastics.

What does a polymer scientist do?

I work with different materials to make them better. Materials can cause problems. I try to solve the problems.

What is one problem that polymer scientists are working on?

Some polymers take years to break down. This makes a lot of garbage. Scientists want to make polymers that break down faster so there is less garbage.

Now It's Your Turn!

▶ **What question would you ask?**

_____

_____

_____

_____

Polymer Play

▶ Think about what a polymer scientist studies. Make a list of polymers on the lines below.

rubber ball

foam peanuts

plastic toy

plastic bags

1 Rubber ball

2 _____

3 _____

4 _____

 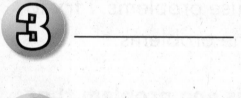  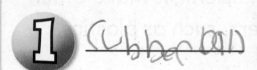

Fun Fact

A lobster's shell is a polymer.

Motion

Big Idea 12

Motion of Objects

Big Idea 13

Forces and Changes in Motion

Florida Marlins batter

I Wonder Why

The ball changes direction when the batter hits it. Why?
Turn the page to find out.

Here's Why The ball changes direction because of the force from the bat.

Track Your Progress

Essential Questions and Florida Benchmarks

LESSON 1 »

How Do Objects Move? 145
SC.1.P.12.1 Demonstrate and describe the various ways that objects can move, such as in a straight line, zigzag, back-and-forth, round-and-round, fast, and slow.

LESSON 2 »
Inquiry

How Can We Move a Ball? 153
Inquiry Flipchart p. 19
SC.1.P.12.1, SC.1.N.1.1, SC.1.N.1.2, SC.1.N.1.3, SC.1.N.1.4

LESSON 3 »

How Can We Change the Way Objects Move? 155
SC.1.P.13.1 Demonstrate that the way to change the motion of an object is by applying a push or a pull.

LESSON 4 »
Inquiry

How Can We Change Motion? 167
Inquiry Flipchart p. 21
SC.1.P.13.1, SC.1.N.1.1, SC.1.N.1.3

People in Science:
Isaac Newton 169
SC.1.P.13.1

Unit 5 Benchmark Review 171

Big Idea 12 *There are many things around you that move. When something moves, you can see it and describe it.*

Big Idea 13 *Forces, or pushes and pulls, can change the way something moves. A force can come from you or from something around you.*

Now I Get the Big Idea!

SC.1.P.12.1 Demonstrate and describe the various ways that objects can move, such as in a straight line, zigzag, back-and-forth, round-and-round, fast, and slow.

Essential Question

How Do Objects Move?

Engage Your Brain!

Find the answer to the question in the lesson.

These Ferris wheel lights look blurry when they are in motion.

How does this Ferris wheel move?

_____

Active Reading

Lesson Vocabulary

1 Preview the lesson.

2 Write the 2 vocabulary terms here.

_____   _____

Set Things in Motion

The log ride climbs up the hill slowly.

log ride

Look at all of the things in motion! **Motion** is movement. When something is in motion, it is moving.

Planes fly fast. A turtle walks slowly. **Speed** is the measure of how fast something moves.

▶ Circle two things that move fast. Draw an X on two things that move slowly.

The log ride zooms down the hill fast.

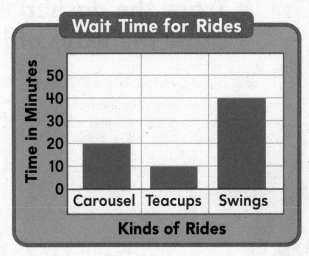

Do the Math!
Make a Bar Graph

Pam went on three rides. This graph shows how long she waited for each ride.

Wait Time for Rides

Time in Minutes

	Carousel	Teacups	Swings
50			
40			40
30			
20	20		
10		10	
0			

Kinds of Rides

Use the graph to answer the questions.

1. Which ride had the shortest wait?

_____

2. How does the graph tell you?

_____

It's Your Move!

Objects can move in many ways.
They can move in a straight line, zigzag,
back and forth, or round and round.

▶ **Trace the dashed lines below to show the ways objects can move.**

straight line

zigzag

Active Reading

A detail is a fact about a main idea. Draw one line under a detail. Draw an arrow to the main idea it tells about.

back and forth

round and round

Sum It Up!

① Draw It!

Read the label in each box.
Draw an arrow to show the kind of motion.

back and forth

zigzag

round and round

straight line

② Circle It!

Look at each pair of objects.
Circle the one that goes fast.

Brain Check

Name _____

Word Play

Work your way through the maze to match the word with its meaning.

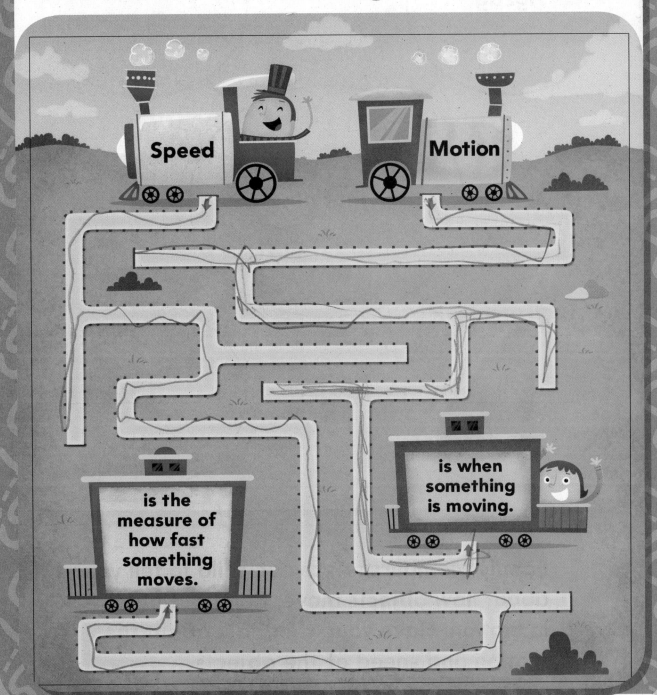

Speed

Motion

is the measure of how fast something moves.

is when something is moving.

Apply Concepts

Complete the word web below.

The Way Things Move

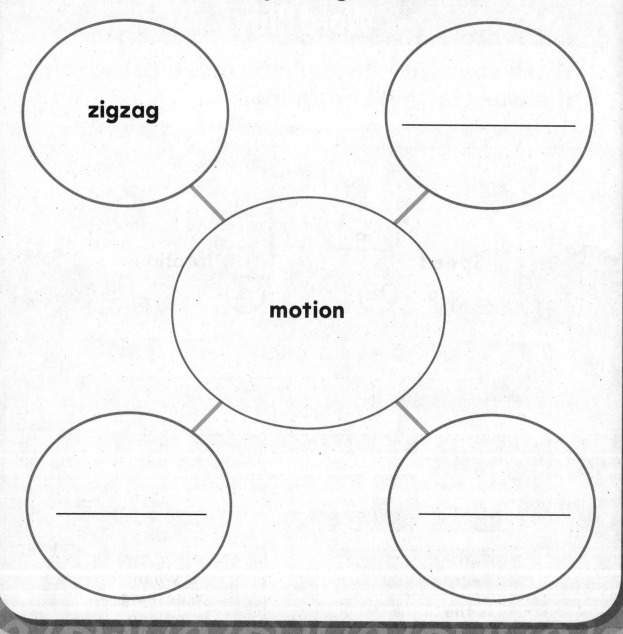

zigzag

_____

motion

_____

_____

Family Members: Ask your child to tell you about how objects move. Point out objects in motion. Have your child talk about the motion and speed of the objects.

Take It Home!

SC.1.N.1.1 Raise questions ... investigate them in teams ... and generate appropriate explanations based on those explorations. SC.1.N.1.2 Using the five senses ... make careful observations ... and compare their observations with others. SC.1.N.1.3 Keep records as appropriate .... SC.1.N.1.4 Ask "how do you know?" .... SC.1.P.12.1 Demonstrate and describe the various ways that objects can move ....

Name _____

Essential Question

How Can We Move a Ball?

Set a Purpose

Tell what you will do in this investigation.

_____

Think About the Procedure

1 What kinds of motion will you show?

_____

_____

2 How will you show the motion?

_____

_____

Record Your Data

Draw what you did.

Motion	Drawing
Straight line	
Zigzag	
Back and forth	
Round and round	

Draw Conclusions

How can a ball move? How do you know?

_____

_____

_____

Ask More Questions

What questions can you ask about how objects move?

_____

_____

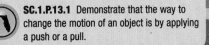
SC.1.P.13.1 Demonstrate that the way to change the motion of an object is by applying a push or a pull.

Lesson 3

Essential Question

How Can We Change the Way Objects Move?

Find the answer to the question in the lesson.

How is pushing a swing like pulling a wagon?

A push and a pull are both

_____ .

Active Reading

Lesson Vocabulary

1 Preview the lesson.

2 Write the 3 vocabulary terms here.

_____   _____

_____

In Full Force

What makes the wagon move? The girl gives it a push. A **push** moves an object away from you. The boy gives the wagon a pull. A **pull** moves an object closer to you.

Pushes and pulls are forces. A **force** makes an object move or stop moving. When the girl and boy push and pull the wagon, it starts to move.

▶ **Draw yourself pushing something.**

▶ Draw yourself
pulling something.

Active Reading

Find the sentence that tells the meaning
of **force**. Draw a line under the sentence.

Using Force

Look at the pictures. How does a force move a ball? A force can change the way an object moves. It can change a ball's speed or direction.

Changing Speed

Force can change an object's speed. It can make something start moving or stop moving. It can make something go faster or more slowly.

▶ **What is going to happen to the ball?**

_____

_____

You can kick a ball to make it start moving or go faster.

You can catch
a ball to stop it.

▶ Describe how the motion of the car changes.

1

2

3

1 _____

2 _____

3 _____

What Is Your Position?

Look at the pictures. Things are moving up and down. They are moving in and out. Position words tell where something is. Some position words are **in**, **out**, **up**, **down**, **left**, and **right**.

A force can move something to a new position.

Active Reading

A detail is a fact about a main idea. Draw one line under a detail. Draw an arrow to the main idea it tells about.

up

down

in

out

A Step in the Right Direction

Think about pushing a friend on a swing. Your friend moves away from you and then comes back. Forces can move things toward you and away from you. A force can change the direction of an object.

▶ **Tell how the direction of this swing changes.**

_____

_____

_____

What Makes That Coaster Move?

Roller coasters are fun! They go up and down, fast and slow, round and round. People on the ride might yell as they change speed and direction. What makes the coaster move?

A motor pulls a chain. The chain pulls the car up the first hill.

Gravity is the force that
pulls the car down.
Gravity pulls all things
toward Earth.

▶ **What pulls the car
down the hill?**

_____

Sum It Up!

① Solve It!

Write the word that solves the riddle.

I move a box
when it is full.
I can be
a push or a pull.
       What am I?

_____

② Circle It!

Forces can change objects. Circle the words that tell the kinds of changes.

speed   color

size   direction

shape

③ Label It!

Write push or pull to label each picture.

pull

push

Word Play

Complete the letter by using these words.

speed	push	force	pull

Dear Jen,

We moved into our new house. My dad drove the moving truck. He made sure the _____ of the truck was not too fast.

Moving is hard! I had to _____ boxes all day. It took a huge _____ to move my box of toys. My dad had to _____ it while my brother pushed.

Your friend,

Amy

Apply Concepts

Complete the chart. Write a word on each blank line.

Cause	Effect
Force	moves a _____.
Force	makes a wagon go _____.
Force	pushes a swing _____ from you.
Force	moves a book to a new _____ on a shelf.

© Houghton Mifflin Harcourt Publishing Company

SC.1.N.1.1 Raise questions ... investigate them in teams ... and generate appropriate explanations based on those explorations. **SC.1.N.1.3** Keep records as appropriate .... **SC.1.P.13.1** Demonstrate that the way to change the motion of an object is by applying a push or a pull.

Name _____

Essential Question

How Can We Change Motion?

Set a Purpose

Tell what you want to figure out in this activity.

_____

_____

Think About the Procedure

❶ What do you want to do to the cube?

_____

❷ List some ideas for how to push the cube.

_____

_____

❸ List some ideas for how to pull the cube.

_____

Record Your Data

Write or draw to show what you did.

Action	What I Did
Push	
Pull	

Draw Conclusions

How do the string, straw, and stick change the motion of the cube?

_____

_____

_____

Ask More Questions

What are some other questions you could ask about changing the motion of a cube?

_____

_____

_____

SC.1.P.13.1 Demonstrate that the way to change the motion of an object is by applying a push or a pull.

People in Science

1

He is known for observing an apple falling from a tree.

2

He wrote his Three Laws of Motion.

4

Things to Know About

Isaac Newton

3

His laws help us understand why things move the way they do.

4

He was one of the greatest scientists in history.

Objects in Motion

▶ Think about what you know about Isaac Newton. Then write the answer to each question.

What did Isaac Newton write after seeing an apple fall from a tree?

he ngh

dowpc

What is Isaac Newton remembered as?

_____

_____

What do the Three Laws of Motion tell us?

_____

_____

UNIT 6
Living Things

Big Idea 14

Organization and Development of Living Organisms

ruby-throated hummingbird

I Wonder Why
This hummingbird sounds like it is humming. Why?
Turn the page to find out.

Here's Why Hummingbirds can flap their wings up to 200 times a minute. The rapid flapping makes the humming sound.

Track Your Progress

Essential Questions and Florida Benchmarks

LESSON 1 »

What Are Living and Nonliving Things?...175
SC.1.L.14.1 Make observations of living things and their environment using the five senses.
SC.1.L.14.3 Differentiate between living and nonliving things.

LESSON 2 »

How Are Plants Different? 185
SC.1.L.14.1, SC.1.L.14.2, SC.1.L.14.3

LESSON 3 »

How Are Animals Different?............195
SC.1.L.14.1, SC.1.L.14.3

LESSON 4 »
Inquiry

What Can Your Senses Tell You About Living Things? 207
Inquiry Flipchart p. 25
SC.1.N.1.1, SC.1.N.1.2, SC.1.N.1.3, SC.1.L.14.1, SC.1.L.14.3

LESSON 5 »

What Are Some Parts of Plants?........209
SC.1.L.14.2 Identify the major parts of plants, including stem, roots, leaves, and flowers.

People in Science:
Lue Gim Gong 219
SC.1.L.14.2

Unit 6 Benchmark Review...............221

Big Idea 14 *Plants and animals are alike and different. They both have parts that help them live. We can observe to learn more.*

Now I Get the Big Idea!

SC.1.L.14.1 Make observations of living things and their environment using the five senses. **SC.1.L.14.3** Differentiate between living and nonliving things.

Lesson **1**

Essential Question

What Are Living and Nonliving Things?

Engage Your Brain!

Find the answer to the question in the lesson.

What do all living things need?

_____

Active Reading

Lesson Vocabulary

1 Preview the lesson.

2 Write the 4 vocabulary terms here.

_____ _____

_____ _____

Living It Up!

Living things are people, animals, and plants. They need food, water, air, and space to live. They grow and change. Living things **reproduce**. They make new living things like themselves.

COW

flowers

▶ **Label the living things you see in the picture.**

BCiD

farme

Dog

SheP

groundhog

What's Nonliving?

Nonliving things do not need food, air, and water. They do not grow and change. What are some nonliving things? A rock is a nonliving thing. Air and water are nonliving things, too.

Active Reading

Find the sentences that tell the meaning of **nonliving things**. Draw a line under them.

▶ **List nonliving things you see.**

Gluvs

shovl

mower

All Together

All the living and nonliving things in a place make up an **environment**. A farm is one environment. It has living and nonliving things.

Active Reading

The main idea is the most important idea about something. Draw two lines under the main idea.

▶ List living and nonliving things you see in a farm environment.

Living	Nonliving
pigs	
sheb chiks hors hen	

Sum It Up!

① Choose It!

Circle each living thing.
Draw an X on each nonliving thing.

② Draw It!

Draw a living thing and a nonliving thing you might find in a park.

Name _____

Word Play

Color the living things. Circle the nonliving things.

Apply Concepts

Complete the chart. Show how living and nonliving things are different.

Living Things	Nonliving Things
1 grow and change	do not grow and change
2 _____	do not reproduce
3 need air	do not need _____
4 need _____	do not need water
5 need food	do not need _____

Look around your environment. Name one living thing and one nonliving thing.

Living Thing	Nonliving Thing
6 _____	7 _____

Family Members: Take a survey of your home with your child. List the living things and the nonliving things you see.

SC.1.L.14.1 Make observations of living things and their environment using the five senses.
SC.1.L.14.2 Identify the major parts of plants, including stem, roots, leaves, and flowers.
SC.1.L.14.3 Differentiate between living and nonliving things.

Essential Question

How Are Plants Different?

Engage Your Brain!

Find the answer to the question in the lesson.

How is this plant like some animals?

_____

_____

Active Reading

Lesson Vocabulary

1 Preview the lesson.

2 Write the 2 vocabulary terms here.

_____ _____

Is It a Plant?

Plants are living things, like animals. Plants are also different from animals.

Plants can not move like animals. They stay in one place. Green plants use light, water, and air to make their own food. Animals eat plants or other animals.

Active Reading

When you compare things, you find out ways they are alike. Draw triangles around two things that are being compared.

Plants and Animals

▶ Complete the chart to tell how plants and animals are different.

	Plants	Animals
make their own food	✓	
eat plants or animals		✓
move around on their own		✓
grow and change	✓	✓

A Venus flytrap is a strange plant. It moves its leaves to catch insects and spiders. Then it eats what it catches.

Plenty of Plants

How can you tell plants apart? They have different leaves. They have different shapes. They can be big or small. Some plants have soft, thin stems. Some have thick, woody stems.

Trees
- tall
- woody trunk
- many branches
- different leaves
- long life

oak tree

Shrubs

- shorter than trees
- smaller, woody stems
- smaller branches
- different leaves
- long life

boxwood shrub

Grasses

- small plants
- soft stems
- long, thin leaves
- shorter life

ornamental grasses

▶ Circle the names of the plants with woody stems. Draw a line under the name of the plant with soft stems.

Plants with Flowers

Some plants have flowers. **Flowers** make a plant's seeds. Flowers can grow on small plants. They can also grow on shrubs and trees. Where have you seen flowers?

hibiscus plant

▶ **What do flowers do?**

seen flowers can grow

Plants with Cones

Some plants have cones. **Cones** hold a plant's seeds. Cones grow on some trees. Where have you seen cones?

Active Reading

A detail is a fact about a main idea. Draw one line under a detail. Draw an arrow to the main idea it tells about.

pinecone

pine tree

Sum It Up!

① Circle It!

Circle the plant that has cones.

② Choose It!

Circle each group of words that tells about an animal.

eats plants or animals

makes its own food

grows and changes

moves around on its own

③ Solve It!

Solve the riddle.

Some living things fly.
Some walk, run, or swim.
I do not move on my own.
I stay in one place.

What am I? _____

SC.1.L.14.1 Make observations of living things and their environment using the five senses. **SC.1.L.14.3** Differentiate between living and nonliving things.

Essential Question

How Are Animals Different?

 **Engage Your Brain!**

Find the answer to the question in the lesson.

This animal is not an insect. What is it?

_____

Active Reading

Lesson Vocabulary

1 Preview the lesson.

2 Write the 6 vocabulary terms here.

_____   _____

_____   _____

_____   _____

All Kinds of Animals

Animals have different shapes and sizes. They have body parts that help them move in different ways. Some animals walk and run. Others fly or swim.

Animals have different body coverings. Some have fur or hair. Others have scales or feathers.

Active Reading

Clue words can help you find ways things are different. **Different** is a clue word. Draw a box around this word.

Ways to Group Animals

feathers
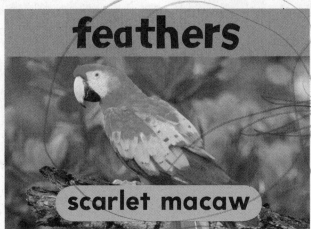
scarlet macaw

fur

spider monkey

swim

river dolphin

climb

red-eyed tree frog

big

capybara

small

leaf-cutter ants

▶ Circle the words that help group animals by the way they move.

golden lion tamarin

giant anteater

Mammals

A **mammal** has fur or hair. Most mammals have live young. A young mammal drinks milk from its mother's body. People are mammals.

▶ Label the body covering you see.

_____

jaguar

quetzal

toucan

Birds

A **bird** has feathers. Birds also have a beak and wings. Most birds use wings to fly. Birds lay eggs. They find food to feed their young.

▶ **Label the body covering you see.**

_____

parrot

Reptiles

A **reptile** has dry skin. It is covered in scales. Most reptiles lay eggs. Most reptiles have four legs. But snakes are reptiles with no legs. Turtles are reptiles. They may have legs or flippers. A turtle also has a shell on its back.

green iguanas

caiman

▶ Label the body covering you see.

_____

Amphibians

Most **amphibians** have smooth, wet skin. Toads are amphibians with rough, bumpy skin.

Amphibians lay their eggs in water. Young amphibians live in the water. Most grown amphibians live on land.

poison dart frog

cane toad

▶ **Label the body covering you see.**

_____

Fish

Fish have body parts that help them live in water. Most **fish** have scales. The scales help keep their bodies safe. Fish have fins to swim. They have gills to take in oxygen.

Active Reading

The main idea is the most important idea about something. Draw two lines under the main idea.

red piranha

silver dollar fish

▶ **Label the body covering you see.**

_____

grasshopper

butterfly

Insects

An **insect** has three body parts and six legs. A hard shell keeps its body safe.

Some animals look like insects, but they are not. A spider has eight legs. It is not an insect.

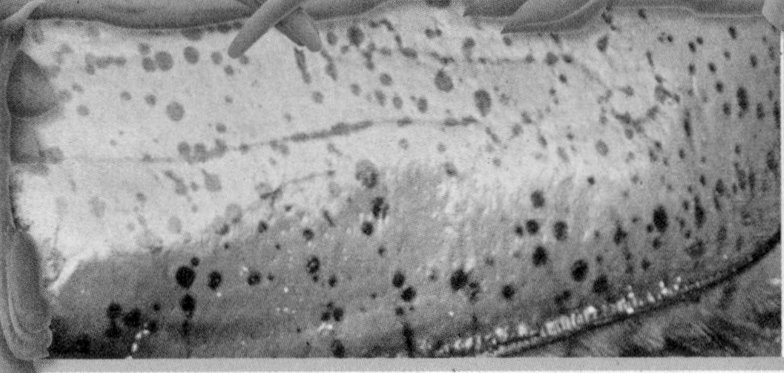

▶ Label the body covering you see.

_____

rhinoceros beetle

Sum It Up!

① Mark It!

Draw an X on the animal that is not a mammal.

Circle the animal that is an amphibian.

② Draw It!

Two animal groups have scales. Draw an animal from each group. Label it.

_____   _____

 **Brain Check**

Name _____

Word Play

Unscramble the letters to name six animal groups.

| reptile | mammal | fish | amphibian | insect | bird |

lammam __ __ __ __ __ __

esctni __ __ __ __ __ __

drib __ __ __ __

phibiaman __ __ __ __ __ __ __ __ __

plitree __ __ __ __ __ __ __

isfh __ __ __ __

Write the circled letters in order to complete the sentence.

There are many different kinds

of _____ .

Apply Concepts

Draw or write an animal from each group.

Animal Groups

Animal Group	Animal from That Group
❶ mammal	
❷ bird	
❸ reptile	
❹ amphibian	
❺ fish	
❻ insect	

Take It Home!

Family Members: Discuss animal groups with your child. Look through magazines and help your child group the animals you see.

SC.1.N.1.1 Raise questions ....
SC.1.N.1.2 Using the five senses ... make careful observations ... and compare their observations with others.
SC.1.N.1.3 Keep records as appropriate ....
SC.1.L.14.1 Make observations of living things and their environment using the five senses.
SC.1.L.14.3 Differentiate between living and nonliving things.

Name _____

Essential Question

What Can Your Senses Tell You About Living Things?

Set a Purpose
Tell what you want to find out.

_____

_____

Think About the Procedure
1 What will you observe?

_____

2 Why will you use a hand lens?

_____

_____

Record Your Data

Record in this chart what you observe.

My Observations	
What I See	
What I Hear	
What I Feel	
What I Smell	

Draw Conclusions

What did you find out about the living things and the environment?

_____

_____

Ask More Questions

What other questions could you ask about living things?

_____

_____

Essential Question

What Are Some Parts of Plants?

Engage Your Brain!

Find the answer to the question in the lesson.

What holds this tree in place?

its _____

Active Reading

Lesson Vocabulary

❶ Preview the lesson.

❷ Write the 6 vocabulary terms here.

_____   _____

_____   _____

A Plant's Makeup

A plant has parts that help it grow and change.

Taking Root

A plant has roots that grow into the soil. The **roots** hold the plant in place. They take in water from the soil. They take in other things from the soil that the plant needs.

roots

Stems Stand Tall

The **stem** holds up the plant. It takes water from the roots to the other parts of the plant.

A flower has a thin, soft stem. A tree has a thick, woody stem.

stems

▶ Draw a triangle around the roots of the bean plant. Draw a circle around the stem.

Leaves at Work

A **leaf** is a plant part that makes food for the plant. It uses light, air, and water.

Active Reading

Find the sentence that tells the meaning of **leaf**. Draw a line under the sentence.

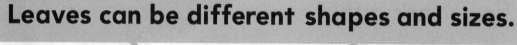

Leaves can be different shapes and sizes.

banana leaf

pine needles

clover

ash

red maple

Flowers, Seeds, and Fruit

Many plants have flowers. A **flower** is a plant part that makes seeds. A new plant may grow from a **seed**. The new plant will look like the plant that made the seed.

Many flowers grow into fruits. A **fruit** holds seeds.

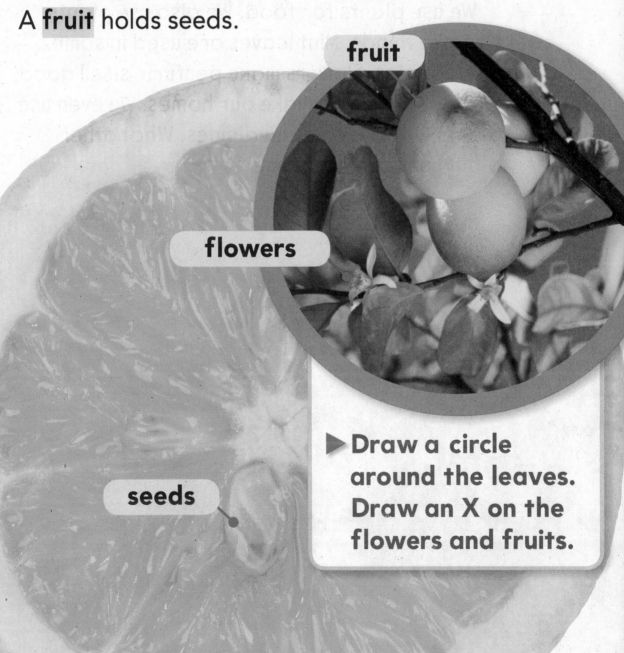

fruit

flowers

seeds

▶ Draw a circle around the leaves. Draw an X on the flowers and fruits.

Plant Power

We use plants for food. We also use plants to make things. Mint leaves are used in some toothpastes. Flowers make perfume smell good. Woody stems help make our homes. We even use plants to make some medicines. What other plant uses can you name?

Do the Math!
Solve a Problem

Look at the tomatoes. Use them to help you solve this problem.

A farmer has 24 tomatoes.
He picks 11 tomatoes.
How many are left?

_____ - _____ = _____

① Choose It!

Circle the plant part that takes in water.

② Solve It!

Solve each riddle.

I can be thick or thin.
I can be short or tall.
I help a plant get
water and hold it up so
it won't fall.

I can be different colors,
shapes, and sizes.
I may fall to the ground.
I take in light and air to
make food for a plant
since it can't move around.

What am I?

What am I?

_____

_____

Name _____

Word Play

Label the parts of the plant.

| flower | leaf | roots | stem |

_____

_____

_____

_____

Apply Concepts

Tell which plant parts the plant needs.

Problem	Solution
❶ I need a plant part to hold seeds. What part do I need?	_____
❷ I need a plant part to take in water. What part do I need?	_____
❸ I need a plant part to make fruit. What part do I need?	_____
❹ I need a plant part to make food. What part do I need?	_____
❺ I need a plant part to hold me up. What part do I need?	_____
❻ I need a plant part to make a plant just like me. What part do I need?	_____

Take It Home!

Family Members: Encourage your child to tell you about the parts of the plant. Help your child name plants you eat and use.

Learn About...
Lue Gim Gong

Lue Gim Gong was born in China. He moved to the United States when he was 12 years old. He spent much of his life in Florida. He did experiments with fruits. His experiments made new fruits. His most famous fruit is called the Lue Gim Gong orange.

Fun Fact

Bees help flowers make new plants.

219

A Lue Gim Gong Time Line

▶ **Use the time line to answer the questions below.**

Lue Gim Gong is born in China.

In his 20s, he grows the first Lue Gim Gong orange.

He comes to the United States as a boy.

Today farmers still grow Lue Gim Gong oranges.

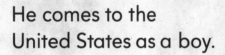

1 Where was Lue Gim Gong born? Draw a box around the name of that country.

2 How old was Lue Gim Gong when he grew his first Lue Gim Gong orange? Draw a triangle around the words that tell you.

3 What do farmers do today? Draw a line under the words that tell you.

Benchmark Review

Multiple Choice

Fill in the circle next to the best answer.

SC.1.L.14.1

1 Which shows animals in an environment?

Ⓐ

Ⓑ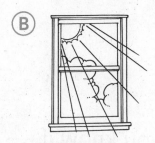

Ⓒ

SC.1.L.14.3

2 You see a living thing that can move on its own. What is it?

Ⓐ an animal

Ⓑ a shrub

Ⓒ a tree

SC.1.L.14.3

3 What kinds of young animals drink milk from their mothers' bodies?

Ⓐ birds

Ⓑ mammals

Ⓒ reptiles

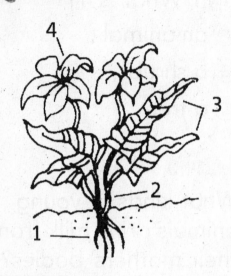

SC.1.L.14.2

4 What plant part does Number 3 show?

(A) flower

(B) leaves

(C) roots

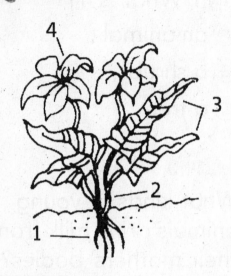

SC.1.L.14.1

5 You count how many times this dog barks.

Which sense do you use to find out?

(A) hearing

(B) smell

(C) touch

SC.1.L.14.3

6 How do you know if something is living?

(A) living things grow, change, and reproduce

(B) living things do not grow, change, and reproduce

(C) living things and nonliving things are the same

Living Things and Their Parents

Big Idea 16

Heredity and Reproduction

Florida panther cub

I Wonder Why

Panther cubs have spots. Why?
Turn the page to find out.

Here's Why Panther cubs are born with dark spots. Spots help a young cub hide. The spots fade as the cub grows older. Then the cub looks more like its parents.

Track Your Progress

Essential Questions and Florida Benchmarks

LESSON 1 »

Which Living Things Look Like Their Parents? 225

SC.1.L.16.1 Make observations that plants and animals closely resemble their parents, but variations exist among individuals within a population.

SC.1.N.1.2 Using the five senses as tools, make careful observations, describe objects in terms of number, shape, texture, size, weight, color, and motion, and compare their observations with others.

Careers in Science:
Zoo Keeper 235

LESSON 2 »

Inquiry

How Are Plants of the Same Kind Different? 237

Inquiry Flipchart p. 28

SC.1.L.16.1 Make observations that plants and animals closely resemble their parents, but variations exist among individuals within a population.

SC.1.N.1.1, SC.1.N.1.2, SC.1.N.1.3

Unit 7 Benchmark Review 239

Big Idea 16 *Young plants and animals are similar to their parents and each other.*

Now I Get the Big Idea!

Essential Question

Which Living Things Look Like Their Parents?

Engage Your Brain!

Find the answer to the question in the lesson.

When is a butterfly not like a butterfly?

When it is a

_____caterpillar_____.

Active Reading

Lesson Vocabulary

1 Preview the lesson.

2 Write the 2 vocabulary terms here.

_____parent_____   _____trait_____

Look Alikes

A **parent** is an animal or a plant that makes young like itself. Parent plants make new plants like themselves. Young plants grow to look like their parents. A **trait** is a feature young plants get from their parents. Pointed leaves and red flowers are traits.

Plants

Parent	Young
strawberry plant	young strawberry plant
▶ Draw an adult plant.	▶ Draw its young.

Adult animals make young animals like themselves. Most young animals look like their parents. Their traits come from their parents. But not all young animals look like their parents. For example, a caterpillar must change to look like a butterfly.

Active Reading

Draw triangles around two things that are being compared.

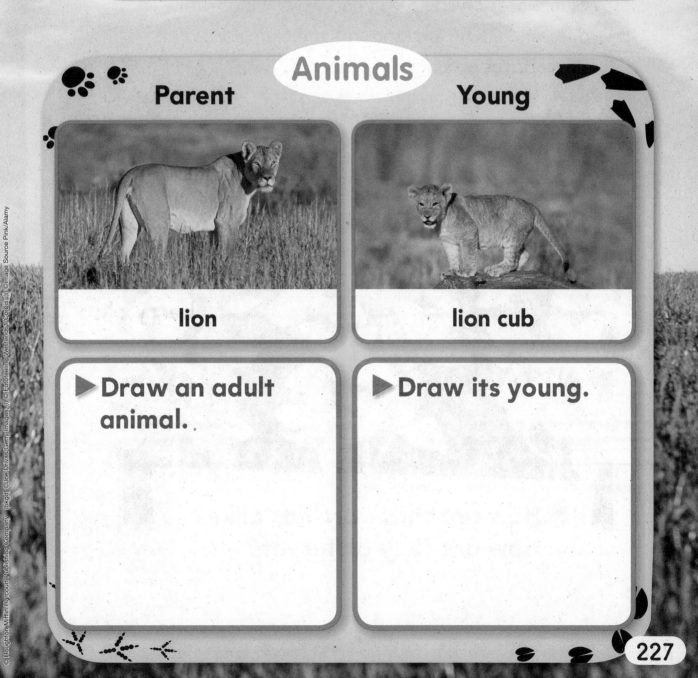

Animals

Parent	Young
lion	lion cub
▶ Draw an adult animal.	▶ Draw its young.

Being Different

Plants of the same kind look alike. But they are also different. They may have the same leaves but different colored flowers. One may grow tall. Another may be short.

Active Reading

Clue words can help you find ways things are different. **Different** and **but** are clue words. Draw boxes around these words.

▶ How are these orchids alike? How are they different?

Animals of the same kind can be different, too. They may have different markings. They may be different colors. They may not behave in the same way. One may run fast. Another may move slowly.

Why is it helpful that things of the same kind have differences?

Appaloosa horses have different markings.

▶**Read the caption. Circle the word that tells how these horses are different.**

Can You Spot the Spots?

Do you know what kind of puppies these are? They are Dalmatians. People know Dalmatians by their white bodies and black spots. Look closely. Are all the dogs the same? No! Each dog looks a bit different from the others. The dogs do not behave the same. The different traits help you tell the dogs apart.

Do the Math!

Make a Bar Graph

You can describe objects by number.

How many puppies have these traits?

Fill in the tally chart.

black on ears	
black spots	
pink around nose	

Use the data to make a bar graph.

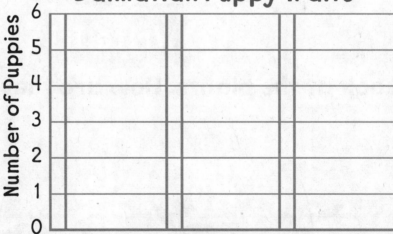

Dalmatian Puppy Traits

Number of Puppies

6
5
4
3
2
1
0

Black ears   Black spots   Pink nose

Puppy Traits

Sum It Up!

① Draw It!

Look at the first cat. Color the second cat so it looks different.

② Write It!

Look at the plants. How are they different?

_____

_____

232

 **Brain Check**

Name _____

Word Play

Find these words in the puzzle.

| trait | spots | parent | color | fast | slow |

```
c  t  o  f  a  s  t
p  a  r  e  n  t  o
t  a  g  l  d  e  i
e  j  s  l  o  w  b
t  r  a  i  t  i  l
k  e  m  e  o  a  d
r  s  p  o  t  s  y
g  f  c  o  l  o  r
```

Write two words to complete the sentences.

1 A living thing that makes young like itself is
a _____ .

2 A feature we get from our parents is
a _____ .

Apply Concepts

Think about what you learned about animal traits. Complete the page.

1 Draw a picture of an animal you might see near your home.

2 Draw a picture of what its young would look like.

3 Think about the animals you drew. How might other animals like this one look or behave differently?

_____

_____

Take It Home!

Family Members: Discuss with your child traits plants and animals may get from their parents. Then talk about traits a child you know has inherited from his or her parents.

SC.1.L.17.1 Through observation, recognize that all plants and animals... need the basic necessities of air, water, food, and space.

Careers in Science

Ask a Zoo Keeper

What does a zoo keeper do?

I feed the animals. I give them water. I make sure that the animals are healthy. I also keep their environments clean.

How do you know when an animal is sick?

Animals can not tell me when they don't feel well. So I observe them carefully. Sometimes an animal eats or moves very little. That could be a sign that the animal is sick.

What else does a zoo keeper do?

I talk to people about the zoo animals. I have fun talking to children. They like animals so much!

Now It's Your Turn!

► What question would you ask a zoo keeper?

_____

_____

Careers in Science *continued*

Now You Be a Zoo Keeper!

▶ **A tiger cub was born at your zoo. Make a plan to take care of the cub.**

My Zoo Keeper Plan

1 I will _____ _____ .

2 I will _____ _____ .

3 I will _____ _____ .

Name _____

Essential Question

How Are Plants of the Same Kind Different?

SC.1.N.1.1 Raise questions ... investigate them in teams ... and generate appropriate explanations based on those explorations. SC.1.N.1.2 Using the five senses ... make careful observations, describe objects in terms of number ... and compare their observations with others. SC.1.N.1.3 Keep records as appropriate .... SC.1.L.16.1 Make observations that plants and animals closely resemble their parents but variations exist among individuals within a population.

Set a Purpose

Tell what you want to find out.

_____

_____

Think About the Procedure

1 What will you observe?

_____

_____

2 What differences will you look for?

_____

_____

Record Your Data

In this chart, record what you observe.

My Observations of Two Plants

	Plant A	Plant B
How the roots look		
How many leaves		
Other observations		

Draw Conclusions

How can plants of the same kind be different?

_____

_____

_____

Ask More Questions

What other questions could you ask about the same kind of plant?

_____

_____

Name _____

Multiple Choice

Fill in the circle next to the best answer.

SC.1.L.16.1

1 Which animal is **most likely** the parent of this animal?

Ⓐ

Ⓑ

Ⓒ

SC.1.L.16.1

2 Which plant could be a young sunflower's parent?

Ⓐ

Ⓑ

Ⓒ

SC.1.L.16.1

3 What will you observe if you look at a row of rosebushes in a garden?

Ⓐ All the bushes are exactly the same.

Ⓑ Each bush is totally different from the others.

Ⓒ Each bush is similar to the others.

SC.1.L.16.1

4 A plant has rounded leaves and pink flowers. What is **most likely** true about the plant's parent?

Ⓐ It has pointed leaves.

Ⓑ It has rounded leaves.

Ⓒ It has spiky leaves.

SC.1.L.16.1

5 Which plant can you conclude is the parent of this plant?

Ⓐ

Ⓑ

Ⓒ

UNIT 8
Plant and Animal Needs

Big Idea 17

Interdependence

spoonbill carrying a twig

I Wonder Why
This bird is carrying a twig. Why?
Turn the page to find out.

Here's Why A spoonbill builds its nest from sticks and twigs. The nest is a safe place for the spoonbill's chicks.

Track Your Progress

Essential Questions and Florida Benchmarks

LESSON 1 »

What Do Plants Need? 243

SC.1.L.17.1 Through observation, recognize that all plants and animals, including humans, need the basic necessities of air, water, food, and space.

LESSON 2 »

Inquiry

Why Do Plants Grow? 253

Inquiry Flipchart p. 30

SC.1.L.17.1 Through observation, recognize that all plants and animals, including humans, need the basic necessities of air, water, food, and space.

SC.1.N.1.1, SC.1.N.1.3, SC.1.N.1.4

People in Science:
Norma Alcantar 255

SC.1.L.14.2 Identify the major parts of plants, including stem, roots, leaves, and flowers.

SC.1.L.17.1 Through observation, recognize that all plants and animals, including humans, need the basic necessities of air, water, food, and space.

LESSON 3 »

What Do Animals Need? 257

SC.1.L.17.1 Through observation, recognize that all plants and animals, including humans, need the basic necessities of air, water, food, and space.

Unit 8 Benchmark Review 269

Big Idea 17 *Plants, animals, and humans need each other to survive.*

Now I Get the Big Idea!

SC.1.L.17.1 Through observation, recognize that all plants . . . need the basic necessities of air, water, food, and space.

Essential Question

What Do Plants Need?

Find the answer to the question in the lesson.

How does this plant grow without soil?

Its roots take in

_____

_____ .

Active Reading

Lesson Vocabulary

1 Preview the lesson.

2 Write the 2 vocabulary terms here.

_____   _____

Plant Needs

Sunlight, Air, and Water

A plant needs certain things to live and grow. A plant needs **sunlight**, or light from the sun. It needs air and water. A plant uses these things to make its food.

Active Reading

The main idea is the most important idea about something. Draw two lines under the main idea.

Air is all around, even though we can not see it.

Plants grow toward the sun to get the sunlight they need.

Plants get most of the water they need from the soil.

▶ **Circle three words that name things a plant needs.**

From the Soil

Most plants need soil to grow. **Soil** is made up of small pieces of rock and once-living things. A plant's roots take in water from the soil.

Some plants do not grow in soil. They live and grow on other plants. Their roots take in rain and water from the air.

Active Reading

A detail is a fact about a main idea. Draw one line under a detail. Draw an arrow to the main idea it tells about.

Space to Grow

As a plant grows, its stem gets taller. Its roots get bigger. It grows more leaves, too. A plant must have enough space to grow.

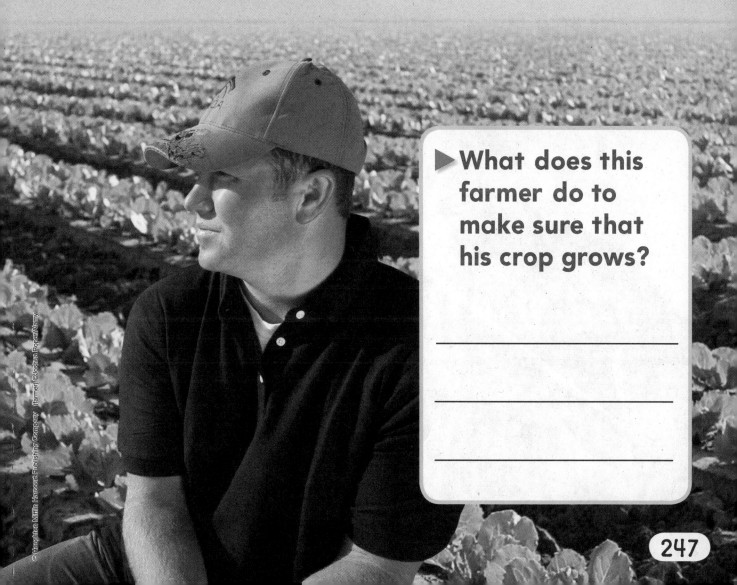

▶ **What does this farmer do to make sure that his crop grows?**

_____

_____

_____

People Helping Plants

How do people help plants? They water plants. They pull weeds so plants have space to grow. People put plants by windows so they can get sunlight.

Active Reading

Clue words can help you find an effect. **So** is a clue word. Draw a box around **so**.

People also help plants by planting new ones. They plant seeds so new flowers can grow. They plant young trees so people can enjoy them.

▶**How do you help plants?**

_____

_____

Sum It Up!

① Circle It!

Circle two things that a plant needs.

② Write It!

This plant has gotten too big for its pot.

What need is not being met?

_____

Name _____

Word Play

Color in the words that name things a plant needs.

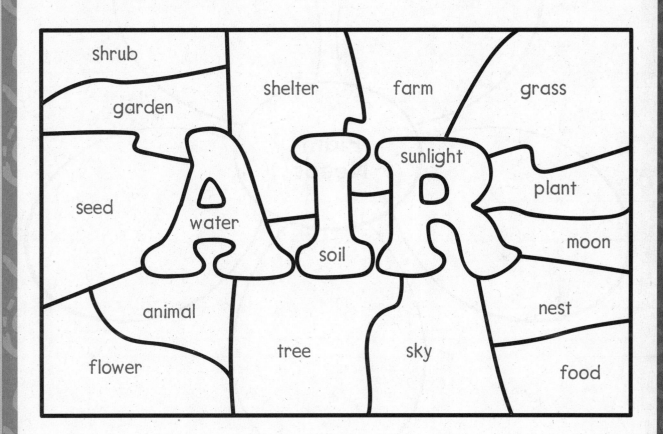

shrub

garden

shelter   farm   grass

seed

AIR

sunlight

plant

water

soil

moon

animal

nest

flower   tree   sky   food

Now answer the question.

What is all around us?

_____

Complete the web to tell what plants need to grow and be healthy.

Plant Needs

Family Members: Ask your child to tell you about the things a plant needs to grow and be healthy. Talk about how your family or someone your family knows helps plants.

SC.1.N.1.1 Raise questions . . . .
SC.1.N.1.3 Keep records . . . .
SC.1.N.1.4 Ask "how do you know?" . . . .
SC.1.L.17.1 Through observation, recognize that all plants . . . need the basic necessities of air, water, food, and space.

Name _____

Essential Question
Why Do Plants Grow?

Set a Purpose
Tell what you want to find out.

_____

_____

Think About the Procedure
1 What will you observe?

_____

_____

2 How will you treat the plants differently?

_____

_____

Record Your Data

In this chart, record what you observe.

My Observations of Two Plants		
	Plant A	**Plant B**
How the stems look		
How the leaves look		
Other observations		

Draw Conclusions

Can a plant grow when it does not get what it needs?

_____

_____

Ask More Questions

What other questions could you ask about plant needs?

_____

_____

Get to Know ...
Dr. Norma Alcantar

Dr. Norma Alcantar studies materials. She makes them more useful. Dr. Alcantar wanted to find a way to make water clean.

She learned that some people in Mexico used prickly pear cactus plants to clean water. The plants have a gooey material. Dr. Alcantar studied it. She used the goo to make water clean.

Fun Fact

She learned about using this kind of cactus from her grandmother.

Clean It!

▶ **Answer the questions about Dr. Alcantar's work.**

1

What does Dr. Alcantar's study?

_____

_____

_____

2

Where did Dr. Alcantar get the idea for using the prickly pear cactus in her studies?

_____

_____

3

Why is Dr. Alcantar's work important?

_____

_____

_____

4

What does Dr. Alcantar use from the cactus to make clean water?

_____

Essential Question

What Do Animals Need?

🧠 Engage Your Brain!

Find the answer to the question in the lesson.

Why is a clownfish shelter unusual?

A clownfish lives

_____

Active Reading

Lesson Vocabulary

1 Preview the lesson.

2 Write the 2 vocabulary terms here.

_____ _____

Food and Water

Animals need food and water to grow and stay healthy. Some animals eat plants. Some eat other animals. Still others eat both plants and animals.

Active Reading

The main idea is the most important idea about something. Draw two lines under the main idea.

A deer drinks water.

Air

Animals need oxygen, a gas in air. Land animals use their lungs to breathe in oxygen. Some water animals, like whales, have lungs. They breathe air. Fish do not have lungs. They use **gills** to get oxygen.

A black bear uses its lungs to breathe.

gills

A fish uses gills to take in oxygen from the water.

▶ Which animal uses its gills to get oxygen?

_____

Shelter

Most animals need shelter. A **shelter** is a place where an animal can be safe. An animal may use a plant as a shelter. It may dig a hole in the ground. It may even use another animal as a shelter. One animal that does this is a clownfish.

Kinds of Animal Shelters

A prairie dog lives in a burrow.

A beaver lives in a lodge.

Some birds lay eggs in a nest.

A skunk lives in a den.

▶ Draw an animal in its shelter.

Space

Animals need space to grow. They need space to move around and find food.

Animals need space for shelter. They need space to take care of their young.

Active Reading

A detail is a fact about a main idea. Draw one line under a detail. Draw an arrow to the main idea it tells about.

A cheetah needs space to run and catch its food.

Your Needs

You are a living thing. You must meet your needs to grow and stay healthy. What do you and other people need? You need air to breathe. You need food and water. You need space and shelter.

▶ **How are the needs of people like the needs of animals?**

_____

_____

Caring for Pets

Pets are animals. Think about some pets you know. Where do they get their food and water? Who gives them shelter? They need people to help them meet their needs.

Taking care of a pet is a big job. A pet needs space to exercise and play. You need to keep the pet and its shelter clean. You must clean up after a pet, too.

People need to take care of pets and keep them clean.

People need to give pets food.

This dog gets 1 cup of dog food in the morning and 1 cup of dog food at night.

How many cups of dog food does it get for 1 day?

1 cup in morning
+ 1 cup at night
_____

_____ cups in one day

How many cups of dog food does it get for 5 days?

_____

Sum It Up!

① Choose It!

Mark an X on the need that does <u>not</u> belong.

Animal Needs

water   sunlight

air   food

② Circle It!

How are people and animals alike?

They both need soil.

They both live in dens.

They both need sunlight.

They both need air and water.

③ Draw It!

Draw the animal you might find in each shelter.

nest	burrow

Name _____

Word Play

Pets need things to help them live and grow.
Fill in the words to tell what a hamster needs.

air   food   shelter   space to grow   water

a_____

w_____

s_____

s_____   f_____

Apply Concepts

Think about how you meet your needs each day. Then fill in the chart below.

You Need	How You Meet Your Needs
① air	_____ _____
② _____	I drink from the water fountain at soccer practice.
③ food	_____ _____
④ _____	I go inside my house when it rains.
⑤ space to grow	_____ _____

Name _____

Multiple Choice

Fill in the circle next to the best answer.

SC.1.L.17.1

1 What do both of these living things need to live?

- Ⓐ air
- Ⓑ rocks
- Ⓒ soil

SC.1.L.17.1

2 What kind of shelter does this animal live in?

- Ⓐ

- Ⓑ

- Ⓒ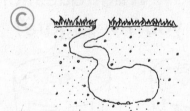

SC.1.L.17.1

3 Which is a reason that plants need sunlight?

- Ⓐ to make water
- Ⓑ to make their own food
- Ⓒ to have space to grow

SC.1.L.17.1

❹ Which part of a plant takes in water from the soil?

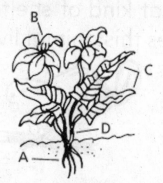

Ⓐ part A

Ⓑ part B

Ⓒ part C

SC.1.L.17.1

❺ You set up two plants this way. What question could you investigate?

Ⓐ Do plants need water to live?

Ⓑ Do plants need light to live?

Ⓒ Do plants need warm air to live?

SC.1.L.17.1

❻ You set up an investigation with four plants of the same kind.

Plant 1 gets light and water.

Plant 2 gets light but no water.

Plant 3 gets water but no light.

Plant 4 gets no water and no light.

Plant 1 grows well. The other plants die. What can you conclude?

Ⓐ Plants need only water to live.

Ⓑ Plants need only light to live.

Ⓒ Plants need both light and water to live.

Interactive Glossary

This Interactive Glossary will help you learn how to spell a vocabulary term. The Glossary will give you the meaning of the term. It will also show you a picture to help you understand what the term means.

Where you see **Your Turn** write your own words or draw your own picture to help you remember what the term means.

A

amphibian

The group of animals that begin life in water. Most grown amphibians live on land. (p. 201)

Your Turn

B

bird

The group of animals with feathers on their bodies and wings. Most birds can fly. (p. 199)

C

cone

The part of a nonflowering plant that holds a plant's seeds. (p. 191)

Interactive Glossary

D

drought
A long time when there is very little rain. (p. 111)

environment
All the living and nonliving things in a place. (p. 180)

E

earthquake
A shaking of Earth's surface. (p. 108)

erosion
A kind of change that happens when wind and water move rock and soil. (p. 110)

Your Turn

energy
Something that causes matter to move or change. Heat and light are forms of energy. (p. 58)

F

fish

The group of animals that live in water and get oxygen through gills. Fish have scales and use fins to swim. (p. 202)

force

Something that makes an object move or stop moving. (p. 156)

Your Turn

flood

A kind of change that happens when streams, rivers, or lakes get too full. (p. 109)

fruit

The part of the plant that holds seeds. (p. 213)

flower

The plant part that makes seeds. (pp. 190, 213)

Interactive Glossary

G

gills
The parts of a fish that take in oxygen from the water. (p. 259)

gills

gravity
A force that pulls things down to Earth. (p. 70)

H

heat
Energy that makes things warmer. It moves from something warmer to something cooler. (p. 59)

I

inquiry skills
Skills that help you find out information. (p. 18)

compare   observe

insect
A kind of animal that has three body parts and six legs. (p. 203)

investigation

A test that scientists do.
(p. 30)

light

Energy that lets us see.
(p. 58)

L

lake

A body of fresh water with land all around it.
(p. 97)

living things

Things that are living. People, animals, and plants are living things because they need food, water, air, and space to live. They grow, change, and reproduce. (p. 176)

Your Turn

leaf

The part of a plant that makes food for the plant. A leaf uses light, air, and water to make food.
(p. 212)

Interactive Glossary

M

magnify
To make something look bigger. (p. 50)

Your Turn

mammal
The group of animals with fur or hair on their bodies. (p. 198)

matter
Anything that takes up space. (p. 124)

moon
A large sphere, or ball, of rock in the sky. (p. 48)

motion
Movement. When something is in motion, it is moving. (p. 146)

N

natural resource
Anything from nature that people can use. (p. 84)

Your Turn

nonliving things
Things that are not alive. They do not need food, air, and water. They do not grow and change. (p. 178)

O

ocean
A large body of salty water. (p. 98)

P

parent
An animal or a plant that makes young like itself. (p. 226)

property
What something is like. Color, size, and shape are each a property. (p. 126)

Interactive Glossary

pull
To move an object closer to you. (p. 156)

push
To move an object away from you. (p. 156)

R

reproduce
To make new living things like oneself. (p. 176)

reptile
The group of animals with dry skin covered in scales. (p. 200)

Your Turn

river
A large body of flowing water. (p. 96)

rock

A hard thing that comes from Earth. (p. 88)

seed

The part of a plant that new plants grow from. (p. 213)

Your Turn

roots

The part of a plant that holds the plant in place. The roots take in water. (p. 210)

S

senses

The way you observe and learn. The five senses are sight, hearing, smell, taste, and touch. (p. 4)

science tools

Tools people use to find out about things. (p. 8)

Interactive Glossary

shelter
A place where an animal can be safe. (p. 260)

soil
The top layer of Earth. It is made up of small pieces of rock and once-living things. (pp. 89, 246)

speed
The measure of how fast something moves. (p. 146)

star
An object in the sky that gives off its own light. The sun is the star closest to Earth. (p. 46)

stem
The part of a plant that holds up the plant. (p. 211)

T

stream
A small body of flowing water. (p. 96)

sun
The star closest to Earth. (p. 46)

sunlight
Light that comes from the sun. (p. 244)

telescope
A tool that helps magnify things in the sky. (p. 50)

temperature
A measure of how warm something is. (p. 129)

Your Turn

Interactive Glossary

texture
What an object feels like. (p. 126)

trait
A feature that young get from their parents. (p. 226)

Your Turn

W

weathering
A kind of change that happens when wind and water break down rock into smaller pieces. (p. 110)

V

volcano
A place where hot melted rock comes out of the ground onto Earth's surface. (p. 108)

weight
How heavy an object feels. (p. 128)

Index

A

Active Reading. *See also* **Reading Skills**
clue words, 70, 196, 228, 248
main idea and details, 4, 32, 34, 46, 60, 84, 98, 100, 110, 124, 149, 160, 180, 191, 202, 210, 212, 244, 246, 258, 262
Air
for animals, 259, 266–267
as natural resource, 84, 92
for plants, 244, 252
Alcantar, Norma, 255–256
Amphibians, 205–206
cane toad, 201
poison dart frog, 201, 204
red-eyed tree frog, 197
Anderson, Mary, 39–40
Animals, 186, 196. *See also* **Amphibians; Birds; Fish; Insects; Mammals; Reptiles**
air for, 259, 266–267
caring for, 264–265
comparison to plants, 187, 194
feathers, 197, 199
food for, 258, 266–267
fur, 197–198
grouping, 196, 206
as natural resources, 86, 90, 92
needs of, 258–262, 267
oxygen for, 259
of same kind, 229
shelter for, 260–261, 267
space for, 262, 267
traits of, 227, 230, 234
water for, 258, 266–267
young and their parents, 227

B

Bacon-Bercey, June, 117–118
Balance, 9, 14. *See also* **Science tools**
Bar graph, 147, 231
Birds, 177, 205–206
feathers, 197, 199
hummingbird, 173–174
nest, 261
parrot, 199
quetzal, 199
scarlet macaw, 197
spoonbill, 241
toucan, 199, 204
Blizzard, 118
Body parts, used with senses, 5, 13
Boxwood shrub, 189

C

Careers in Science
inventor, 39–40
meteorologist, 117–118
polymer scientist, 139–140
zoo keeper, 235–236
Cause and Effect, 166
Classify, 20, 24–26
Clouds, 46, 54
Communicate, 20, 24, 26, 33
Compare, 18, 25–26
Cones, 191–193

D

Daytime sky, 46, 52. *See also* **Nighttime sky**
clouds, 46, 54
moon, 45–46, 48, 51, 53–54
sun, 46, 54

© Houghton Mifflin Harcourt Publishing Company

Index

Do the Math!
  compare solid shapes, 49
  make a bar graph, 147, 231
  measure length, 11
  model fractions, 99
  order by weight, 128
  solve a problem, 73, 215, 265
Draw Conclusions, 22, 26, 28, 33, 56, 94, 136, 138, 154, 168, 208, 238, 254
Drought, 111, 115

Earth, 76, 99
Earthquake, 108, 115–116
Energy, 65
  heat, 59, 65
  light, 58, 60, 65
Environment, 180–181
Erosion, 110, 115–116

F

Farm as environment, 180–181
Fish, 205–206
  clownfish, 260
  gills, 259
  red piranha, 202
  silver dollar fish, 202, 204
Float
  draw conclusions, 136
  objects, 135
  record data, 136
Flood, 108–109, 115–116
Florida
  beach, 81, 121
  Marlins, 143
  panther, 223
  ruby-throated hummingbird, 173
  spoonbill, 241
  Tampa, Museum of Science and Industry, 1
Flowers, 176, 190, 193, 213–214, 217–218
Food for animals, 258, 266–267
Force, 164, 166
  cause and effect, 166
  changing direction, 161, 164
  changing position, 160, 164, 166
  changing speed, 158, 164
  gravity, 163
  pulling, 157
  pushing, 156, 166
  roller coasters, 162
  using, 158
Fresh water, 105
  lake, 97, 104–105
  river, 96
  stream, 96
Fruit, 213, 218

Galilei, Galileo, 77–78
Gills, 259
Gong, Lue Gim, 219–220
Gravity
  force, 163
  pulling, 70–71, 74–76
  pushing against, 72–73, 75–76

Hand lens, 8, 12, 14. *See also* **Science tools**
Heat, 59, 65
Hibiscus plant, 190
Hurricane, 118
Hypothesize, 21, 26, 31, 37

Infer, 22, 25–26
Inquiry Skills

classify, 20, 24–26

communicate, 20, 24, 26, 33

compare, 18, 25–26

draw conclusions, 22, 26, 28, 33, 56, 94, 136, 138, 154, 168, 208, 238, 254

hypothesize, 21, 26, 31, 37

infer, 22, 25–26

make a model, 23–24, 26

make a plan, 21, 31

measure, 8–12, 14, 19, 25–26, 129, 137–138

observe, 12, 18, 25–26, 30, 37, 54, 56, 93–94, 208

plan investigation, 21, 24–26

predict, 19, 24–26

record data, 28, 34, 37, 56, 94, 136, 138, 154, 168, 208, 238, 254

sequence, 23–26

using, 26–28

Insects, 203–206

butterfly, 203

grasshopper, 203

hard shell, 203

leaf-cutter ants, 197,

204

rhinoceros beetle, 203

Investigation, 37

do the test, 32

draw conclusions, 33

hypothesize, 21, 26, 31, 37

make a plan, 21, 31

observe, 12, 25–26, 30, 37

record, 34, 37

Kearns, Robert, 40

Lakes, 97, 104–105

Leaf, 212, 216–218

ash, 212

banana, 212

clover, 212

mint, 214

pine needles, 212

red maple, 212

Light, 58, 60, 65

Lightning, 118

Living things, 176, 182–183. *See also*

Animals; Plants

animals, 186

bird, 177

comparison to

nonliving things, 184

cow, 176

dog, 177

draw conclusions, 208

in farm environment, 181

flowers, 176, 182, 193

groundhog, 177

plants, 186

reproduce, 176

senses about, 207–208

sheep, 177

tree, 177

Lungs, 259

Magnifiers

draw conclusions, 56

hand lens, 8, 12, 14

record data, 56

telescope, 50–53, 77–78

work of, 55–56

Magnify, 50, 53

Main Idea and Details, 4, 32, 34, 46, 60, 84, 98, 100, 110, 124, 149, 160, 180, 191, 202, 210, 212, 244, 246, 258, 262

Mammals, 198, 205–206

Index

Appaloosa horses, 229

bear, 259

beaver, 260

capybara, 197, 204

cheetah, 262

cow, 91

Dalmatians, 230

deer, 258

Florida panther, 223

fur, 197–198

giant anteater, 198, 204

golden lion tamarin, 198

jaguar, 198, 204

lion, 227

prairie dog, 260

river dolphin, 197

skunk, 261

sloth, 196

spider monkey, 197, 204

tiger cub, 236

Mathematics Skills. *See* **Do the Math!**

Matter, 124–125

air, 124

property of, 126

Measure, 19, 25–26

length, 11

liquids, 9

science tools for, 8–12, 14

temperature, 129, 137–138

Measuring cup, 9, 12, 14. *See also* **Science tools**

Melting, 61

Meteorologist, 117–118

Moon, 45–46, 48, 51, 53–54

shape of, 49

Motion, 146, 150–152

changing, 167–168

draw conclusions, 154, 168

laws of, 170

objects in, 170

record data, 154, 168

Museum of Science and Industry, Tampa, 1

Natural resource, 85, 90

air, 84, 92

animals, 86, 90, 92

plants, 86, 92

rocks, 88, 90, 92

soil, 89–90, 92

water, 85, 90, 92

Newton, Isaac, 169–170

three laws of motion, 170

Nighttime sky, 48, 52

clouds, 54

moon, 48, 54

observe, 54

Nonliving things, 182–184. *See also* **Living things**

air, 178

characteristics of, 178

comparison to living things, 184

in environments, 180–182

water, 178

Object movement, 148, 151

Observe, 12, 18, 25–26, 30, 36–37, 54

nighttime sky, 54

record data, 56, 208

rocks, 93–94

Ocean, 98, 104–105

Orchids, 228

Ornamental grasses, 189

Oxygen for animals, 259

Parents, 226–227, 233
People, needs of, 263, 268
People in Science
    Alcantar, Norma, 255–256
    Anderson, Mary, 39–40
    Bacon-Bercey, June, 117–118
    Galilei, Galileo, 77–78
    Gong, Lue Gim, 219–220
    Kearns, Robert, 40
    Newton, Isaac, 169–170
Pets
    caring for, 264–265
    needs of, 267
Pine tree, 191. *See also* **Cones**
Plan investigation, 21, 24–26
Plants, 86, 186. *See also* **Animals**
    air for, 244, 252
    apple, 91
    boxwood shrub, 189

    characteristics differences, 232
    comparison to animals, 187, 194
    cones, 191–193
    draw conclusions, 238, 254
    flowers, 190, 213–214, 217–218
    fruit, 213, 218
    hibiscus plant, 190
    leaf, 212, 217–218
    as natural resources, 86, 92
    needs of, 244–247
    oak tree, 188
    orchids, 228
    ornamental grasses, 189
    people helping, 248–249
    pine tree, 191
    record data, 238, 254
    roots, 210–211, 217–218
    of same kind, 228, 237–238
    seed, 213, 218
    soil for, 245–246, 252
    space to grow, 247, 250, 252
    stem, 211, 217–218
    strawberry, 226

    sunlight for, 244–245, 252
    traits of, 226
    use of, 214
    water for, 244–246, 252
    young and their parents, 226
Polymers, 139–140
Polymer scientist, 139–140
Predict, 19, 24–26
Property of matter, 126, 133
    color, 127
    shape, 126
    size, 126
    temperature, 129
    texture, 126–127
Pull, 75, 156, 164–165
Push, 156, 164–165

R

Reading Skills
    cause and effect, 166
    draw conclusions, 22, 26, 28, 33, 56, 94, 136, 138, 154, 168, 208, 238, 254
    main idea and details, 4, 32, 34, 46, 60, 84, 98, 100, 110,

Index

124, 149, 160, 180,
191, 202, 210, 212,
244, 246, 258, 262
sequence, 23–26
Record data, 28, 34,
37, 56, 94, 136, 138,
154, 168, 208, 238, 254
Red maple, 212
Reproduce, 176
Reptiles, 205–206
caiman, 200
green iguana, 200
River, 96, 104–105
Rock, 178
draw conclusions, 94
as a natural resource,
88, 90, 92
observe, 93–94
properties of, 88, 94
record data, 94
Roots, 210–211, 217–218
Ruler, 9, 12, 14. *See also*
Science tools

S

Salty water. *See* **Ocean**
Science tools
balance, 9, 14
hand lens, 8, 12, 14
measuring cup, 9, 12,
14
ruler, 9, 12, 14

tape measure, 9, 12,
14
thermometer, 9, 12
Seed, 213, 218
Senses, 4, 13, 16
body parts for, 5, 13
hearing, 6, 13
seeing, 7, 13
smelling, 7, 13
tasting, 7, 13
touching, 6, 13
using, 15–16
Sequence, 23–26
Shapes, 132
as a property, 126
Shelter
for animals, 260–261,
267
burrow, 260, 266
den, 261
lodge, 260
nest, 261, 266
Shrub, 193
boxwood, 189
Sink
draw conclusions, 136
objects, 135
record data, 136
Size, as a property,
126

Sky
clouds, 54
daytime, 46, 52, 54
moon, 48, 54
nighttime, 48, 52, 54
shapes of objects, 49
star, 46, 49, 52–54
sun, 46, 53–54, 65
Soil
as a natural resource,
89–90, 92
for plants, 245–246,
252
Speed, 146, 151, 165
Spiders, 187, 195, 203
Star, 46, 49, 52–54
Stem, 211, 216–218
Storm, 118
Strawberry plants, 226
Stream, 96, 104–105
comparison to lakes,
97
Sun, 46, 53–54, 57,
64–66
heat, 59
light, 58, 60
melting, 61
staying safe in, 62–64
Sunglasses, 63
Sunlight for plants,
244–245, 252
Sunscreen, 63, 65

T

Tampa, Museum of Science and Industry, 1

Tape measure, 9, 12, 14. *See also* **Science tools**

Telescope, 50–53
Galilei, Galileo, 77–78

Temperature, 133
draw conclusions, 138
measure, 129, 137–138
as a property, 129
record data, 138

Texture, 126–127, 133

Thermometer, 9, 12. *See also* **Science tools**

Thunder, 118

Tornado, 118

Traits, 233
of animals, 227, 230, 234
of plants, 226

Turtles, 200

V

Venus flytrap, 187

Volcano, 108, 115
erupting, 109

W

Water
for animals, 258, 266–267
bathing, 85
drinking, 85
fresh, 96–97, 104–105
as a natural resource, 85, 90, 92
ocean, 98, 104–105
for plants, 244–246, 252
protecting, 101
staying safe in, 103
traveling in, 85
watering plants, 85

Water safety, 102

Weathering, 110, 113, 116

Weight, 128, 133

Why It Matters, 10, 50, 72, 102, 130, 214, 230, 264–265

Z

Zoo keeper, 235–236